2 Corinthians

Books in the Bible Study Commentary Series

*Not yet published as of this printing.

BIBLE STUDY COMMENTARY

2 Corinthians

Aída Besançon Spencer,
William David Spencer

Lamplighter
Books Grand Rapids,
Michigan
Zondervan Publishing House

Dedicated with love
to our wonderful son Stephen

BIBLE STUDY COMMENTARY: SECOND CORINTHIANS
Copyright © 1989 by Aída Besançon Spencer and Willian David Spencer

Lamplighter books are published by Zondervan Publishing House
1415 Lake Dr., S.E., Grand Rapids, MI 49506

Library of Congress Cataloging-in-Publication Data

Spencer, Aída Besançon.
    Second Corinthians / by Aída Besançon Spencer and William David
Spencer.
      p. cm. — (Bible study commentary)
    "Lamplighter books."
    Bibliography: p.
    ISBN 0-310-36101-X
    1. Bible. N.T. Corinthians, 2nd—Commentaries. I. Spencer, William David,
1947– . II. Title. III. Series: Bible study commentary series.
  BS2675.3.S64 1989
  227′.307–dc20   89-31722
                                                      CIP

If not the author's own translation, then Scripture quotations are taken from the
Holy Bible: New International Version (North American Edition), copyright ©
1973, 1978, 1984 by The International Bible Society. Used by permission of
Zondervan Bible Publishers.

Scripture quotations marked RSV are taken from the Revised Standard Version,
copyright © 1946, 1952, 1971 by the Division of Christian Education of the
National Council of the Churches of Christ in the United States of America.

Scripture quotations marked KJV are taken from the King James Version of the
Bible.

While the publisher recognizes and believes in the equality of the sexes, in the
interest of easy readability, the convention of using male pronouns has been
observed. Simplicity and consistency will be best served by this grammatical
decision.

Edited by John D. Sloan, Mary McCormick

Printed in the United States of America

89 90 91 92 93 94 / CH / 10 9 8 7 6 5 4 3 2 1

Contents

Pilgrim in Autumn

Stripping down for winter
    like trees lightening their loads,
Dropping golden leaves like extra pounds,
Shaking off the summer excess
    to a fighting trim,
Looking now to take fierce winter on,

Training fills the streets and yards with beauty,
Giving wealth away without regret,
Before the spring of plenty and recovery,
There will be a desperate fighting yet,

When every bit of strength needs to be marshalled,
And no bit of frippery has the luxury to stay,
In tolling the eleventh hour when other sounds
are quelled,
Shedding off what ties us to today,

Staunchly in the winter twilight,
Gently into that good night,
Reaching for the blessing sun,
And God's glorious "well done."

                —William David Spencer

Preface

Second Corinthians is perhaps the most discouraging yet encouraging letter of Paul the apostle in the entire New Testament. For poor Paul, the church he helped found at Corinth set new lows in Christian living that must have been terribly depressing. One crass but provoking way to examine a New Testament letter is to ask—did it work? Did the people to whom it was written take its advice and straighten out their faith and practice? Second Corinthians is our proof that Paul's advice in 1 Corinthians had not been totally heeded. Many of the same sins he had warned the church at Corinth to discontinue were still being committed, and Paul finds he must write another letter immediately after his previous one, even more firmly begging the Corinthians to mend their spiritual ways. Paul must have been deeply disturbed that not only had the advice God gave him a year before been largely ignored, but now even his position as advice-giver to the Corinthians was also being challenged by outsiders.

At the same time, 2 Corinthians is for us Christians perhaps the most encouraging epistle of all times in the New Testament. We sometimes find ourselves weighed down emotionally when we reflect on the sheer weight of the horrible things we do. Our brightest members fall into gross, publicly-mocked sexual sins. We are greedy with our resources and stingy in sharing them with others, often contentious and battling among ourselves, looking more like combatants than community members. We are riddled with horoscopes and other silly superstitions. We are a rebellious lot, starving the true leaders God raises up in our churches and fawning over some glittering fraud with a silver tongue and a shifty eye. All of these sins the Corinthian Christians were guilty of committing. And not only did they commit them, but they also continued to sin after they had been warned by God through Paul to stop. Yet neither God nor his minister Paul abandoned them and closed their church. God persisted in loving these foolish, worldly followers until—most encouraging and delightful of all—God's and Paul's persistence paid off handsomely. Second Corinthians was a letter that worked. Its advice was heeded. The Corinthians mended their ways.

For today's Christians no better decision could be made than to invest time in serious study of the passionate, life-giving, epistolary drama of God's reconciliation with humanity that is 2 Corinthians. To gain the very best benefit one can from the following commentary, we recommend that you read the Letter of 2 Corinthians in its entirety *before* using the commentary. This is a crucial step. Your reading will allow you to get a sense of the sweep of the argument, seeing a purpose flow through the content as a whole. Second Corinthians is often misunderstood as a compilation of jumbled thoughts—a smorgasbord of Paul's "oh-and-I-forgot-to-tell-you-abouts" tossed together. Such is far from the case. Our goal is to help the reader grasp the overall argument of the letter and enter into the mind of the original writer. If possible in your initial reading, try to discover Paul's main exhortation to his readers, the one in which he takes into account their needs and problems.

Second Corinthians is a wonderful living document, poignant and passionate as it traces God's intervention within a living relationship between a team of ministers and a church. It reads like one of the great epistolary novels that have been so popular in literature from the early days of Samuel Richardson's *Clarissa* to today's searing *The Color Purple* by Alice Walker. Because theology in action is its theme, 2 Corinthians is as exciting as a theological novel. But best of all, it is authentically true—a real record of God's dealing with God's people.

One of the challenges facing commentators is to determine the best way to open a book to the reader. We prayed and puzzled together about 2 Corinthians: Should we study it verse by verse? Paragraph by paragraph? Theme by theme? The present commentary series is designed for the informed lay reader (though it is also of great benefit to pastors and students). What would lay readers coming to our commentary want as they prepare to teach a Bible study class, or seek enrichment for their own personal or family devotions? Given the strict size limitations of each volume in this particular series, and since the major problem for any reader in approaching 2 Corinthians is in seeing how each of its seemingly unrelated parts connects, we concluded that tracing the flow of Paul's argument, and filling our pages with helpful information and insights that readers can use as tools to understand Paul's points was best.

Toward this end we have concentrated on answering these questions in each section: Why did Paul put in this particular content? What insights can we get from the specific words he chooses? What are their meanings, especially in the rest of the New Testament? What are the key words and phrases? What are the divisions in each passage? What does a passage *not* mean? What are common misconceptions? What different interpretations do others have? What light can be shed from archaeology, from ancient Greco-Roman and Jewish writers, and from the early church fathers, the disciples of the disciples? What further study can one do? Finally, what is the relevance for today, for our spiritual lives, for our church, and our world?

Our study was done in the original Greek text. Along with our translations, we employed the New International Version (NIV) as the main translation in which to record biblical quotations for the reader. A study Bible such as the NIV Study Bible, which includes a brief verse by verse commentary, might be a helpful supplement. Translations other than the NIV or our own are indicated in parentheses. The important thing for the reader to remember, however, is that each passage from Scripture should be digested before any secondary literature such as this or any other commentary will be of benefit. Let the author of the text, the Holy Spirit, first speak to you—then counsel together with us as we mutually explore the text.

Second Corinthians is perhaps the most human book in the New Testament. Appropriately, there are several crucially important people the authors would like to acknowledge. Dr. Cullen Story first introduced Aída to the critical study of

2 Corinthians in 1971 and Dr. Earle Ellis introduced William in 1975. Dr. Story had a keen grasp on the nature of the book, and, interestingly, had his class read novels by Dostoyevsky such as *Crime and Punishment* and *The House of the Dead* as companion pieces. Further, Aída would like to thank her students in the classes she has taught in 2 Corinthians over the years at Gordon-Conwell Theological Seminary in South Hamilton, Massachusetts. The bulk of the material is drawn from her teaching notes. Steven James Weibley, a Byington student Scholar at Gordon-Conwell, researched several key images in the original Greco-Roman and Jewish sources: Who carried the spice in a parade? How did Philo use "tent"? He was of immeasurable help. She would also like to thank Dr. John Polhill of the Southern Baptist Theological Seminary in Louisville, Kentucky, who supervised her doctoral studies in 2 Corinthians, and Allan Fisher and the Evangelical Theological Society who helped these become the book *Paul's Literary Style: A Stylistic and Historical Comparison of 2 Corinthians 11:16–12:13, Romans 8:9–39*, and *Philippians 3:2–4:13* (Eisenbrauns). William would also like to thank his students in "Theology of the Early Church Fathers and Mothers" at Gordon-Conwell in which he taught 1 Clement and the foreground of 2 Corinthians; editors Mark Lau Branson and C. René Padilla whose *Conflict and Context: Hermeneutics in the Americas* published his and Aída's paper on 1 and 2 Corinthians from the Theological Students Fellowship's and Latin American Theological Fraternity's "Context and Hermeneutics in the Americas Conference"; and Grace Chapel's Adult Enrichment Series, Lexington, Massachusetts, for whom he was able to teach a lay class on the Corinthian correspondence. Both of us warmly thank president Robert Cooly and Gordon-Conwell for Aída's sabbatical, which allowed her time to write, and Eagle's Wings Tours who helped arrange our trip to Corinth during the writing of this commentary. Exploring the ruins firsthand opened up many insights. Returning from Corinth, we were welcomed and aided by the Seminario Evangelico of San Juan, Puerto Rico, where we completed the manuscript. John Sloan, Ed van der Maas, and the staff at Zondervan gave us the opportunity to do the study along with encouragement and aid along the way. Chris Smith, faculty secretary at

Gordon-Conwell, quickly and accurately typed the manuscript into the computer. Finally, there is a key person whom we must acknowledge and to whom we would like to dedicate this commentary.

For the last several months our home and our church life have been dominated by our studies in 2 Corinthians. Our ten-year-old son Steve has been one of our chief wellwishers, taking great responsibility to let us work, keeping his friends in iron line, helping in any way he can. Today he stopped Dad on the stairs and asked, "Can I help write the book? I'll do it for free." Children know when they are loved, and an attraction that pours out of 2 Corinthians is the love of Paul for his two beloved children in Christ, Timothy and Titus—and through them, ministry for all his dear but erring family at Corinth. Years ago when Steve was still small, Dad wrote him his very own poem.

For Stephen
I had a little bird.
I kept it in my pocket,
And felt its heart against my chest,
A watch within a locket.
I had a little furry ball.
It was a little mouse.
It hurried, scurried here and there,
All around the house.
I had a little puppy.
It was roly-poly sweet.
And every time it tried to play,
It tangled in its feet.
I have a little boy,
Leaping in the leaves,
Who hides and scurries roly-poly,
Just like all of these.

—Dad

Today Steve is a young man, growing in faith and in power like the first Stephen, the great deacon whose courage in the face of martyrdom so impressed Saul. Paul the apostle loved all his spiritual children dearly, and that love shines through 2 Corinthians. Someday, no doubt, he will be delighted when he learns that a commentary on his letter was dedicated to another fine young Christian man.

Introduction

The Corinthian letters have from the beginning (as far as our written records indicate) been considered authentic and canonical (a "reed" or rule by which we can measure our lives). Clement of Rome, before the end of the first century, writes to the Corinthians and refers to the letter Paul wrote them against factions at the beginning of Paul's preaching ministry (I Clement 47:1–2). Polycarp, the Bishop of Smyrna, who was martyred in A.D. 155, quotes from 2 Corinthians several times in his letter to the Philippians (2:2; 6:1–2; 11:3), as does Irenaeus. The early church historian Eusebius of Caesarea indicates that in the third century the church "recognized" Paul's epistles as true and genuine (*History of the Church* 3:25), and no wonder, since 2 Corinthians is written from "Paul, an apostle" and it is full of personal references.

Unity of 2 Corinthians

Nevertheless, since the Enlightenment, some people have wondered indeed how many letters Paul has written to the Corinthians, what the nature was of Paul's opponents at Corinth, especially compared to the nature of adversaries at other churches, and whether 2 Corinthians 6:14–7:1 was written by Paul. Since Paul's opponents are first explicitly mentioned in chapter 10, we will summarize what we know about them when we come to that chapter.

We need to know before we start to study, however, whether we can treat 2 Corinthians as one document. Johann

Salomo Semler first postulated in 1776 that 2 Corinthians was originally several letters (chs. 1–9 were one (or more) letters; chs. 10–13 were another). Other writers have suggested that 2 Corinthians was originally four or six letters sent not in the same order as we now have in our Bibles (1:3–2:13; 7:5–16 [one letter]; 2:14–6:13; 7:2–4 [one letter]; 6:14–7:1 [one letter]; ch. 8 [one letter]; ch. 9 [one letter]; chs. 10–13 [one letter]). Reconstructing the sequence and occasion for such a series of letters can become a joint task for a historical *and* a mathematical genius.

Notwithstanding, the different tones and themes in 2 Corinthians do cause notice in our era when educated people are taught that objective truth should be separated from passion. How can Paul be thanking God in 9:15 but entreating the Corinthians in 10:1? The "super-apostles" (11:5; 12:11) are not mentioned until chapters 10–13. In addition, the reader needs to invest some thought to coordinate the historical events Paul cites. Paul speaks about going to Macedonia in 2:13, but does not return to this topic until 7:5. Verse 6:13 seems to precede 7:2 better than it does 6:14. Chapter 9 seems to repeat chapter 8.

Although these observations are true, is postulating several letters the best answer? Some people have thought that Paul simply wrote in the midst of interruptions. We have noticed that Paul tends in several of his letters to change his tone as he discusses a particular topic, even as today someone might say, "Don't get George off on the topic of his being fired from work because you'll never hear the end of it!" Paul becomes more brusque whenever he begins to speak about those opponents who have dedicated themselves to undermining his whole ministry, because he becomes righteously angry against sin (e.g., 2 Cor. 10:1; Phil 3:2; Rom. 16:17; Gal. 6:12). Moreover, as we read and reread 2 Corinthians with a sympathetic eye, we can notice more and more allusions and threads connecting the fabric of the letter. Although Paul does not directly confront his opponents until chapter 10, from the very first chapter he alludes to them and to the Corinthians' lack of loyalty. Second Corinthians is not a brief, to-the-point administrative memo sent to a dissident employee: "Shape up or ship out!" Rather, it is a subtle, lovingly, passionately well-crafted literary piece—Paul's last attempt after many partial successes (or were they partial failures?) to bring the Corinthians into full repentance and advancement into God's reign (1 Cor. 5:9; 2 Cor. 2:9; 7:8).

Purpose of the Letter

What was the purpose of Paul's well-crafted letter? Paul wrote his letter before he was about to leave for Corinth to warn the Corinthians that they needed to "mend their ways" (RSV; 2 Cor. 12:21–13:10) before his arrival. He also wanted to make sure Titus and the other Christians were well received when they came to ask for the offering for the poor Christians at Jerusalem. Throughout the letter, Paul defends his style of leadership as a godly one in order that the Corinthians may not be misled. Paul mentions his position as an apostle (1:1), especially when people have not fully accepted him.

Structure of the Letter

After his introductory greetings, Paul begins by defending the manner in which he and his associates in ministry have behaved with a pure motive and godly sincerity in the grace of God (1:3–2:17), noting that persons with impure motives would not experience severe afflictions as they had. Moreover, Paul's change of plans was not due to vacillation, but because he wanted to spare the Corinthians another painful visit. Paul wants to impress on the Corinthians that he and his coleaders have been *genuine* servants.

Not only are they sincere, they are also competent because their competence to be ministers of the new spiritual covenant comes from God (3:1–5:21). Paul explains that the Corinthians themselves are proof of Paul's success. These "living letters" are part of a living new covenant written by the Spirit of the living God. Explaining the differences between the two covenants, Paul suggests that the Corinthians may be living under the old, not the new, covenant. Ministers of this new covenant can be frank, and not become discouraged by difficult circumstances. Therefore, the Corinthians can be proud of Paul and his coworkers.

After setting his defense, Paul now becomes more explicit, urging the Corinthians not to accept the grace of God in vain

(6:1–9:15). Paul entreats the Corinthians to "open their hearts" to him and his coworkers because Paul and his associates have wronged no one. Rather, the Corinthians need to be purified. After this strong exhortation, Paul lovingly tells the Corinthians that he has confidence in them. They had followed some of the directions he had given them in a previous letter. They had also become enthusiastic about giving financially to the poor Christians in Jerusalem. However, the Corinthians as well as the Christians throughout their province, Achaia, should *complete* their promise to give generously.

In the last major section of the letter Paul addresses his defense most directly, urging the Corinthians to change their behavior so that he will not have to discipline those people who suspect him of acting in a worldly fashion (10:1–13:11). Paul and his coworkers do not act in a worldly fashion. Again he reminds them of his love and genuineness, exemplified by the suffering he has had to endure. Yes, the Corinthians might very well conclude that Paul and his associates "have been defending" themselves (12:19)—because they were—but Paul repeats that all they do and say is in God's sight and for the maturity of the Corinthians. All the different themes in the letter occur again in the final verses, dramatically illustrated by Christ "crucified in weakness, yet he lives by God's power" (13:4). The paradox of weakness and grace is a key thought for this letter, leaving readers then and readers today with the exhortation to follow Jesus' example and to practice the oft-repeated but seldom-practiced thought, "Do not evaluate people as worthy from a human point of view" (cf. 5:16ff.).

The contents of 2 Corinthians may be outlined as follows:

Purpose: Paul defends his and his coworkers' style of leadership as an honorable one in order that the Corinthians may not be misled.

I. Introductory greetings (1:1–2)
   A. The Writer(s) (1:1a)
   B. The Readers (1:1b–2)
II. Paul's Defense: We Behave Sincerely with Pure Motives in God's Grace (1:3–2:17).
   A. Paul's Team Experiences Afflictions in Asia (1:3–11).

B. Paul's Planning Was Sincere (1:12–2:17).
III. Paul's Explanation: Our Competence Comes from God (3:1–5:21).
   A. God's Covenant Written on Living Hearts Causes Frankness (3:1–18).
   B. God's Mercy Encourages Paul in Hard Times (4:1–5:10).
   C. Corinthians Should Be Proud of Paul and His Team (5:11–21).
IV. Paul's Warning: Do Not Accept God's Grace in Vain (6:1–9:15).
   A. Paul's Plea: Make Room for Us in Your Hearts (6:1–7:3).
   B. Paul Has Confidence in the Corinthians (7:4–9:15).
V. Paul's Warning: Change or Be Disciplined (10:1–13:11).
   A. Paul Defends His Team's Actions as Not Worldly (10:1–11:11).
   B. Paul Explains His Style of Work (11:12–12:18).
   C. Paul Summarizes His Defense (12:19–13:11).
VI. Final Greetings (13:12–14)
   A. Closing Benediction (13:12–14)
   B. Effect of 2 Corinthians (13:14)

For Further Study

1. If not already done, read (or listen on tape to) 2 Corinthians in one sitting, writing down any insights and questions you might have. It may take anywhere from twenty minutes to an hour or more.

2. Read 1 and 2 Corinthians, jotting down the different spiritual and social characteristics of the Christians at Corinth.

3. Read Acts 15:35–21:33 to get background information on Paul's second and third missionary journeys up to his arrest in Jerusalem. If you have the time, read all of Acts. As you read, find on a map the places Paul visited.

Chapter 1

Introductory Greetings
(2 Corinthians 1:1-2)

A. The Writer(s)

1. Paul (1:1a).

Who was Paul? Each year an agnostic Jewish historian at a major United States university stuns his vast Western Civilization lecture section with the statement, "The conversion to Christianity of a man as remarkable as Paul has ever after forced historians to deal seriously with the claims of Christianity. That a man of his caliber could take Jesus Christ seriously means we must, too. You may not accept Jesus' claims, but because of Paul you must consider them if you are truly going to be an historian."

The letter we call Second Corinthians begins both in the Greek text and in our translations with the name of this remarkable person, "Paul, an apostle of Christ Jesus by the will of God." What do we know about this unusual man?

We first come upon him in what might seem a most unlikely setting. An "upstart" named Stephen, one of the hellenized Jews who had all the population in an uproar over their fantastic claims about a recently crucified carpenter from Nazareth, had outraged the Sanhedrin and been rushed from the city for execution. Stoning was done in a ditch about twelve feet deep. One witness would push the condemned into the ditch while two witnesses picked up stones to drop on or hurl at the heart of the unfortunate person. If the condemned did not die, all the crowd would stone him until he did die. Stoning was done for serious religious crimes such as incest, blasphemy, idolatry, desecration of the Sabbath, cursing father or mother, or witch-craft. Customarily, the condemned confessed so that he or she would be redeemed at the resurrection. As a moral lesson, therefore, children were often brought to stonings.

One young man—the term *neanias* in Acts 7:58 applies to a young male adult from about the 24th to the 40th year—stood by approvingly (Acts 8:1). As he guarded the outer coats laid at his feet by excited and sweaty witnesses wanting to free their arms to inflict their justice more fiercely and effectively, how little could he have imagined that someday he, too, would stand in a similar pit falling beneath the stones at Lystra—bearing testi-mony to that same Lord of Glory for whom Stephen died gladly, Jesus the Christ (Acts 14:19). What did he think as Stephen, instead of confessing his sins, called the witnesses guilty and forgave them?

Obviously, he was not initially convinced, but he was stirred, for immediately after Stephen's death we are told the young man Saul set about to destroy the church, entering house after house, carrying off both women as well as men to prison. So fierce was the persecution that Christians were scattered all over while Saul, breathing murderous threats, began pursuing the church as far afield as Damascus in Syria, over 130 miles away (and not by a straight road).

It was there in Damascus that a startled Christian believer named Ananias first witnessed the conversion of the firebreath-ing Hebrew traditionalist Saul to the Christian hellenized Paul. Ananias is told in Acts 9:11 to meet a man of Tarsus, Saul by name. In Acts 21:39 Paul also says about himself, "I am a Jew, from Tarsus in Cilicia." What was this city, Tarsus, that spawned such a history-changing individual as Paul?

a. Tarsus (1:1a). The Cilician plain was very fertile, and Tarsus was the chief city of its eastern part. "Cilicium" means literally "goat's hair," and Tarsus' special industries were the weaving of linen and the making of tents. Silver, lead, and iron were mined from the northern mountains and carried south through Tarsus. Tarsus' residents were proud of the Cilician Gates—for centuries the only major road through their moun-tains. Since 2300 B.C. Tarsus had been an important center of coastal trade, seated some ten miles from the coast, connected by way of the Tarsus or Cydnus River that opened into a lake, the Harbor Rhegma. Its distance inland protected it from pirates, and visitors as notable as Cleopatra, who traveled up the Cydnus about 41 B.C., would visit this politically, economically, and intellectually prominent city. Tarsus may have been mentioned as early as Genesis 10:4. Excavations have recovered architectural objects from before the time of King David. Pompey in 67 B.C. established it as the capital of the united province of Cilicia, which contained both eastern Cilicia and Syria during Paul's lifetime. Anatolians were the natives, but Greek settlers and traders had turned Tarsus into a hellenistic city where Romans and a large Jewish colony jostled each other in the marketplace.

To be counted a citizen of such a thriving city one needed essentially to be an aristocrat, to have property. Therefore, Paul's family had to have had distinction and at least a moderate amount of wealth. In extending citizenship to the distinguished of each race of people, Alexander the Great had achieved his program of hellenization, uniting the oriental and occidental in a harmonious balance. During the Civil War, Mark Anthony, and afterwards Augustus, granted Tarsus the status *civitas libera* (a free city), which assured it local autonomy, no tribute to pay, and a ruler appointed by Rome. Powerful Tarsus was allowed to mint its own coins, and it grew to a thriving city of at least a half-million people, about the size of Boston, or San Juan, or Perth.

The great Cicero, whose enduring works such as *On Moral Obligation (De Officiis)* are still being printed today, was governor of the province in 50 B.C. Aramaic and Greek rippled fluently throughout the healthy hubbub of a sophisticated cosmopolitan center, and its citizens, as Paul (who spoke Greek and Hebrew [Acts 21:37, 40]), were bi- and trilingual. Intellectually, Tarsus was the third university center of the ancient world with Athens and Alexandria, according to the ancient geographer Strabo (Geo. 14.5.13). Tarsus was distinguished by its native interest in learning. Its schools were filled with local students rather than with foreign ones, as were the schools of Alexandria, and among its residents it boasted of the famous Stoic philosopher Athenodorus.

Into this thriving intellectual environment Paul was born to a family whose occupation was a very prominent one in Tarsus: tentmaking. The identifying word *skēnē* usually denotes a tent, temporary shelter, or a house. Chrysostom, Theodoret, and possibly Origen, called Paul a "leather-worker," confusing some into believing that this meant he was not a tentmaker. Most tents were made of leather, however, so the terms would be synonymous, though scholars are in fact not certain what material Paul used in making his tents. If Paul continued to work at his occupation throughout his life, does this mean that his family denounced him, disowning him financially? Philippians 3:8 does say Paul gave up all for Christ. However, every faithful student of the Hebrew law was taught a trade by which to live. As Rabbi Judah b. Ilai (ca. 150 A.D.) lectured, "Whoever does not teach his son a trade teaches him to become a robber." Having been born in Tarsus well endowed Paul with the intellectual, social, and industrial gifts that God would later call him to use.

Still, though born in Tarsus, Paul was reared in Jerusalem, having been given a thorough training. The word employed in Acts 22:3 denotes "strictness, exactness," in learning the law that came from ancestors. So Paul's background was mixed, causing scholars to wonder to what extent Paul's thought was primarily hellenistic or primarily rabbinic. Which one prevailed in his upbringing: Tarsus or Jerusalem? To what extent was he a Greek or a Jew?

b. Paul as a Youth (1:1a). This young man, we are told, according to Acts 13:9, actually had two functional names: "Saul, who was also called Paul." Saul is his Jewish name, Paul his Greco-Roman one. The Holy Spirit, we note in Acts 13:2, calls him Saul, and he is called by that name in 13:9, but thereafter he is called Paul. So, Paul does not appear to be his "Christian" name and Saul his "non-Christian" name, but the former is his name among Gentiles and hellenized Jews, and the latter his name among strict traditional rabbinic Jews.

To what degree was Paul shaped by his experience of being born in Tarsus, but reared in Jerusalem? W. C. Van Unnik in his book *Tarsus or Jerusalem: The City of Paul's Youth* believes Paul spent all the years of his youth in Jerusalem, employing "reared" to mean his upbringing both by his parents and his educators. Elementary education would proceed from ages five to seven through ten or twelve, followed by secondary education, with instruction in rhetoric at the age of fourteen or fifteen. As Aboth 5:21 in the Mishnah teaches, "At five years old [one is fit] for the Scripture, at ten years for the Mishnah, at thirteen for [the fulfilling] of the commandments." Paul himself declares in Acts 26:4 that from his youth everyone in Jerusalem (and among the Jews) knew his manner of life. However, since in Galatians 1:14–16 he notes that God "was pleased to reveal his Son" to him after Paul had persecuted the Church, and in Acts 9:5 he does not recognize Jesus' voice, Paul apparently does not seem to have seen Jesus during Jesus' ministry in Jerusalem. Thus, we cannot be exactly certain when Paul left Tarsus for Jerusalem. It could have been immediately after his birth or as late as at fourteen years of age.

Paul's father, we know, had the rights of a Roman citizen. Although members of a congregation in the diaspora (or dispersion of the Jews from their homeland, Israel) in Tarsus, Paul's parents were legalistic Jews, Pharisees. They taught their son the Torah in Hebrew. And Paul was also acquainted with the Septuagint, the translation of the Hebrew Scriptures into Greek.

c. Paul As A Roman Citizen (1:1a). Born into a family of Roman citizens, Paul inherited their status (Acts 22:28). How his family first obtained their citizenship we do not know. William M. Ramsay in *St. Paul the Traveller and the Roman Citizen* suggests it may have been for distinguished services to the state or as a reward for helping colonize Tarsus.[1] Paul employed the rights of his citizenship to ensure proper trial and proper scourging. These rights included *provocatio*: citizens could appeal to Roman courts (e.g., Acts 25:10–12). Further, citizens could be punished only after having been proven guilty, and they could not be whipped while being questioned,[2] a practice Augustine deplores in *The City of God*, for it killed many innocent people while establishing their innocence (e.g., Acts

---

[1] Ramsay, W. M., *St. Paul the Traveller and the Roman Citizen* (New York: G. P. Putnam's, 1896), p. 32.

[2] Sherwin-White, A. N., *Roman Society and Roman Law in the New Testament* (Oxford: Clarendon, 1963), pp. 58–9.

22:24–29 at Jerusalem; Acts 16:36–38 at Philippi). Citizens could hold public office, marry other citizens, and have their legal and business matters officially protected.

d. Paul as a Hebrew (1:1a). Paul thoroughly establishes his Hebrew credentials in his speeches and correspondence: "I am a Pharisee, the son of a Pharisee" (Acts 23:6–8). The Pharisees were the strictest party of the Jewish religion (Acts 26:5), "of the tribe of Benjamin, a Hebrew of Hebrews" (Phil. 3:5). "Are they Hebrews?" he asks of the so-called "superapostles" in 2 Corinthians 11:22, "So am I. Are they Israelites? So am I." When mistaken for an Egyptian terrorist in Jerusalem,, he displays his credentials, "I am a Jew . . . brought up in this city. Under Gamaliel I was thoroughly trained in the law of our fathers and was just as zealous for God as any of you are today" (Acts 22:3).

Paul's teacher, Gamaliel I, the elder, was the descendant of the renowned Hillel for whom Jewish religious clubs at universities are still named today. He was honored for the gentleness and kindness of his teaching. Head of one of the two major schools of Hebrew thought in Paul's time, Gamaliel I stood in contrast to the school of Shammai, whose teaching was characterized by strictness and sternness. For example, the breach of one law for Shammai is a breach of the whole law, while for Gamaliel I a person was judged by whether good or bad predominated in his life. Gamaliel I's son, Simeon ben Gamaliel I, became a leader of a Pharisaic community in Jerusalem, observing strict rules of admission. According to Joachim Jeremias, Israel boasted only 6,000 Pharisees, while Jerusalem alone had at least 25,000 to 30,000 people in that religious community, including 18,000 priests.[3]

The Pharisees were mainly lay people who wanted to extend the regulations for the priest into everyday life. Their concern was the maintenance of "ritual purity" in their personal lives, extending to their lives in the world. As such, they wielded enormous influence in the synagogue, practicing in daily life separation from ritual uncleanness and unclean persons. Their very name "Pharisee" is a Greek transliteration

---

[3] Joachim Jeremias, *Jerusalem in the Time of Jesus: An Investigation into Economic and Social Conditions during the New Testament Period*, 3rd ed. trans. F. H. and C. H. Cave (Philadelphia: Fortress, 1969), pp. 251–2.

of the Hebrew term *perushim* ("separated"). Heirs of the
Hasideans of 168 B.C. who arose around the Macabbean uprising
in reaction to the hellenizing of the Seleucid rulers, the
Pharisees called themselves "companions." They became colleagues and scholars who stressed the twofold law: written
scriptures and oral tradition. The Pharisees, as we see in the
Gospel accounts, were acutely aware of Jesus, and some Jewish
scholars even believe the teacher R. Eleazar of Modiim refers to
Paul:[4]

> If a man profanes the Hallowed Things (or "the Sabbaths")
> and despises the set feasts and puts his fellow to shame
> publicly and makes void the covenant of Abraham our father,
> and discloses meanings in the Law which are not according to
> the *Halakah*, even though a knowledge of the Law and good
> works are his, he has no share in the world to come (Aboth
> 3:12).

Thus Paul, as a Pharisee and a Roman citizen, was familiar
with the Jews in the diaspora. He hailed from a distinguished
cosmopolitan city, Tarsus, where he worked at the honorable
trade of tentmaking, and had also the double advantage of
spending his youth in Jerusalem, studying under no one less
than the great Gamaliel I. Paul could rightly be proud of his
upbringing, and even if his elementary education were done in
Tarsus not Jerusalem, Paul would not necessarily have had an
extensive pagan background. Often, religious people in an alien
environment are even more strict in the tenets and practices of
their faith than are indigenous residents. And Paul's learning in
the classics may have come not from any pagan but from
Gamaliel, himself, who taught his students the Greek classics
along with their Hebrew learning.

 e. Paul's Personal Characteristics (1:1a). Scholars have
found Paul very difficult to understand and represent. The
second century apocryphal work *Acts of Paul and Thecla*
records, in chapter 3, he was: "a man little of stature, thin-haired
upon the head, crooked in the legs, of good state of body, with
eyebrows joining, and nose somewhat hooked, full of grace: for

---

[4]Joseph Klausner, "What is Paul for the Jews?" *Contemporary Thinking
about Paul: An Anthology*, ed. Thomas S. Kepler (New York: Abingdon-
Cokesbury, 1950), p. 368.

sometimes he appeared like a man, and sometimes he had the face of an angel." From the New Testament we can corroborate, Paul did have a good state of body. In Acts 14:19–20 we see him stoned, dragged, left for dead, then rising and walking both that same day and the next! Was he little of stature? In 2 Corinthians 10:10 he can be maligned: "in person he is unimpressive and his speaking amounts to nothing," even though he spoke frequently, being mistaken for Hermes, the messenger of the gods, in Acts 14:12. So he may very well have been unimposing in height. While he often lectured expressively (gesturing and beckoning to enforce a point, rending his garments, calling with a loud voice), some physical disability (e.g., Gal. 4:13–15; 6:11) checked his efficiency from time to time. However, if this affected his eyes, as most scholars believe, it did not keep Paul from scrutinizing people intently (Acts 13:9; 14:9).

f. Highlights of Paul's Middle Life (1:1a). After his dramatic conversion from persecutor of Christians to persecuted Christian on the Damascus road, Paul sought to understand why he had been chosen. What did the Lord mean in Acts 9:15–16 when he ordered Ananias, "Go! This man is my chosen instrument to carry my name before the Gentiles and their kings and before the people of Israel. I will show him how much he must suffer in my name." Paul invested many days in Damascus (nearly three years), then spent a while in Jerusalem and Tarsus. For at least a year with Barnabas and others he team-taught a large number of converts in Antioch. Acts 9:22 tells us, "Saul grew more and more powerful and baffled the Jews living in Damascus by proving that Jesus is the Christ." Considering himself, as he tells the Corinthians, "one abnormally born" (1 Cor. 15:8), he needed all the time he took (some fourteen years of preparation) to readjust mentally to the new truth he had discovered. At last, while serving at Antioch, he was called with his coworker Barnabas to a special work (Acts 13:2), and he began writing his epistles after being sent out by the church at Antioch, which had become his home assembly. Now he was going to expand the ministry of his apostleship.

g. Paul as an Apostle (1:1a). Originally "apostle" applied to a naval military expedition by ship. It came to mean a group sent forth for a particular person; eventually, an individual sent forth as an envoy with specific orders. By the time of the New Testament an *apostolos* could be simply an invoice, a bill sent with goods, or a passport. The Jews had "apostles" called *shaliach* or "messengers" who could be dispatched to collect tribute owed to the temple, or to bear messages to foreign powers.

To the Christians an apostle was one who was sent forth by Jesus. Paul refers to the Twelve (1 Cor. 15:5; cf. Luke 6:13) as well as "to all the apostles" (1 Cor. 15:7). Paul could claim apostleship in the smaller sense by declaring himself the thirteenth member of the Twelve, representing the Levites, who were not counted among the tribes—or perhaps as God's replacement for Judas instead of the choice the human apostles themselves made. But Paul could rely on the broader definition accepted in the early church from whose ranks the apostles selected Matthias, Judas's replacement. This was one who had seen Jesus (1 Cor. 9:1), usually someone who had accompanied Jesus from the time of his baptism by John to his ascension (Acts 1:21–22). Under this definition such people as James, the Lord's brother and author of the epistle, Barnabas, Silas or Silvanus, Junia, and Andronicus were regarded as apostles, though not members of the original twelve (Acts 14:14; Rom. 16:7; Gal. 1:19; 1 Thess. 1:1; 12:6). The point herein is that such a person was a witness to Jesus' authentic resurrection.

Paul, in a remarkable incident, despite the fact he had not seen Jesus in his earthly ministry, did see Jesus on the Damascus road, conversing with him. Thus Paul, too, could claim he was an apostle, and not one appointed through people (Gal. 1:1). When listing the eyewitnesses to the resurrection, the 500, James, and "all the apostles," he could list himself as the "least" of the apostles (1 Cor. 15:1–10). He could display in his own life and ministry the signs of a true apostle (2 Cor. 12:12), for Jesus himself had appointed Paul to serve and bear witness to the truth (Acts 26:12–18). But not all were disposed to accept Paul's claims. Particularly troublesome was a group claiming the authority of apostleship for themselves. Their dogged fight against Paul, which raged across the battlefield of the churches and centered for one taxing battle at Corinth, threatened to subvert the entire Corinthian church to a new set of superlative apostles and a new wayward teaching making its own hostile claims on the Corinthians. Paul and his coworkers were sorely pressed to combat these impostors, and all the resources of Paul and his partner Timothy were deeply plumbed to serve the Corinthian church.

2. And Timothy Our Brother (1:1a).

Who was Timothy? The son of a Jewish Christian mother and Gentile father (Acts 16:1), Timothy lived in Lystra, where he may have become a believer when Paul on his first missionary journey passed through in Acts 14:6. All the Christians in his hometown had spoken well of him, and Paul wanted Timothy to join his pastoral team. But knowing the opposition of the Jews to having a hellenized Jew for a preaching companion, Paul circumcised Timothy (Acts 16:3), and they traveled together from town to town, ministering to the churches and delivering the decisions the Jerusalem elders had reached for the new churches to follow. Paul left Timothy behind in Berea and Thessalonica to establish the Thessalonians in the faith (Acts 17:14; 1 Thess. 3:2ff.). Timothy's job was to exhort and explain the part that afflictions have in the faith. Timothy was apparently successful, for he was able to bring Paul good news about the Thessalonians' faith (1 Thess. 3:6ff.). Again, with the Corinthians, Timothy is Paul's emissary. Timothy reminds the Corinthians of the ways of Paul and serves himself as a model (1 Cor. 4:16–17). Again he brings news to Paul (1 Cor. 16:10–11). He is with Paul in prison in Rome, when Paul writes to Philemon.

In the same way Paul sends Timothy to strengthen and report on the churches at Thessalonica and Corinth, he plans to send Timothy to the church at Philippi (Phil. 2:19ff.). Timothy, he tells the Philippians, is unique. Paul has on his team no one else as sincerely loving and concerned with the church's welfare as Timothy is. Paul was perhaps instrumental in Timothy's receiving a new birth, and we know he circumcised him. Thus, as a spiritual father to his son, he loves him—as Timothy in turn serves his spiritual parent Paul, and Paul serves Christ. Thus Paul can urge the Philippians to follow his own example while living according to the pattern that both he and Timothy gave them (Phil. 3:17). And he can counsel Timothy as his younger counterpart, modeled on his own style, to take his place, remaining in Ephesus, charging people not to teach false doctrines (1 Tim. 1:3), commanding and teaching and setting a good example for the believers until Paul can come (1 Tim. 4:6, 11; 6:2). These capabilities were given to Timothy through means of prophecy when elders laid commissioning hands upon him (1 Tim. 1:18; 4:14; 2 Tim. 1:6). So Paul knows he has God's seal on his own affection for and trust in Timothy. Timothy is Paul's beloved child, his dear son (2 Tim. 1:2), and Paul urges him to form relationships with other trustworthy, faithful people similar to the one Paul has with him. He, too, is to become a spiritual mentor passing on what Paul has taught him (2 Tim. 2:2), enabling others to become teachers. He is to be constantly reminding them of good faith and practice (2 Tim. 2:14), continually preaching the truth, correcting, rebuking, and encouraging—always with great patience, and with a careful watch on his own doctrine (2 Tim. 4:2).

Timothy is Paul's coworker. The term "coworker" is a technical term for Paul. It comes from two words that signify "working together." When in the dative case, it can simply signify "helper," but in the genitive case (which Paul always employs for specific people) it means "a person of the same trade, colleague." In 1 Corinthians 16:15–16, Paul uses it for a household of ministers, that of Stephanas. Therefore, Paul can order the Corinthians to "be subject to such people and to every coworker and worker" (1 Cor. 16:16). These people are Paul's colleagues, ministering together with him, working side by side in the harvest. Thus Paul can require they be honored as such, adjuring the Corinthians, "therefore, give recognition to such people" (1 Cor. 16:18). Worthy of note is that Paul does not use the gender-specific term *aner* ("male") to describe coworkers here, but the generic masculine pronoun, opening the term to all Christian persons. In Paul's pastoral team, coworking ministers were not only males like Timothy, but also females like Euodia and Syntyche who as "my fellow coworkers" "contended at my side in the cause of the gospel" (Phil. 4:2–3). Interestingly, the literal phrase Paul employs is "fought by my side," and this military imagery is used repeatedly in his correspondence with

Timothy. Paul's ministry was like a war waged. He reminds Timothy of the "persecutions, sufferings—what kinds of things happened to me in Antioch, Iconium and Lystra (Timothy's own home town), the persecutions I endured" (2 Tim. 3:11). Paul would heartily have sung that great Dutch folk hymn of thanksgiving, "We Gather Together" with its ringing words, "We all do extol Thee, Thou Leader triumphant, and pray that Thou still our Defender wilt be." Echoing the victorious promise of Psalm 34:19, "Many are the afflictions of the righteous; but the Lord delivers him out of them all" (RSV), he exclaims, "Yet the Lord rescued me from all of them." Thus, he encourages Timothy. Paul is like a patrol captain under the great commander Jesus. He sends out Timothy as scout to organize the resistance to evil, fortify those stationed at the outposts, and report back to Paul, having received orders to represent his superior in every mode.

This military imagery that Paul constantly employs when speaking to Timothy is striking. "Fight the good fight," he tells him in 1 Timothy 1:18 (literally "wage the good warfare"). And again he exhorts him in slight variation in 1 Timothy 6:12, "Fight the good fight of the faith." In 1 Timothy 4:7–8 he commands, "train yourself to be godly," for he reminds Timothy that "physical training is of some value, but godliness has value for all things . . . ." Does this suggest that Timothy kept himself in fighting trim or had had physical training? We know he is youthful (1 Tim. 4:12), and Paul urges him "to conduct" himself as an example. The word Paul employs (*anastrophē*) is that used for soldiers (the concept coming down to us in our good conduct medals). Paul urges Timothy to keep himself pure (1 Tim. 5:22; also 4:12; 5:2), a necessary order to both the young and to soldiers when on leave. Timothy, we know, had digestive difficulties, and Paul felt it necessary to command him to stop drinking water only and to take in some alcohol, which would treat his "frequent illnesses" (1 Tim. 5:23). Sometimes people represent Timothy as a timid young man, filled with anxiety that kept his stomach in a turmoil, frightened of the ferocious dissidents in the churches and needing to be told again and again to shore up his courage and do his work. But what if Timothy has been misread? Could he perhaps have been a soldier in the Roman army, sent to the east to help garrison the wide empire, who contracted one of the multitudinous stomach disorders that so weakened the far-flung army of Alexander the Great long before Rome sent its legions following in Alexander's soldiers' bootprints? Could he have been honorably discharged because of his chronic disease, keeping himself in military trim until Paul drafted him into the army of Jesus Christ? "Endure hardship with us like a good soldier of Christ Jesus," Paul goes on to command him in 2 Timothy 2:3–5: "No one serving as a soldier gets involved in civilian affairs—he wants to please his commanding officer. Similarly, if anyone competes as an athlete, he does not receive the victor's crown unless he competes according to the rules." Is Paul alluding to images in Timothy's own past? He continues in verses 6 and 7, "The hardworking farmer should be the first to receive a share of the crops." Did Timothy return to civilian life trying to find another occupation before God's "Greetings" arrived? Paul concludes, "Reflect on what I am saying, for the Lord will give you insight into all this." Paul does use military imagery regularly when writing (e.g., 1 Cor. 9:7, 25; 2 Cor. 10:3–4; Col. 1:29; 2:1; 4:12).[5] But to Timothy specifically he writes as his own model to follow: "I have fought the good fight, I have finished the race, I have kept the faith" (2 Tim. 4:7), all relevant admonitions for a young solider/athlete turned minister to keep in mind for his own life. The matter is certainly speculatory, but worthwhile to consider.

A more difficult question to answer is whether, despite the listing of his name in each greeting, Timothy actually was a cowriter of this and the other five letters credited as being from Paul and Timothy: 2 Corinthians, Philippians, Colossians, 1 and 2 Thessalonians, and Philemon. This letter like the others is "from" Paul and Timothy, but does that statement actually infer authorship or simply assent? The question arises in the light of such passages as "I, Paul" (2 Cor. 10:1), "I write these things" (13:10). "For the Son of God, Jesus Christ, who was preached among you by me and Silas and Timothy ... " (not by us coauthors, 1:19) suggests that Paul is the one writing. The use of personal pronouns varies between the first person singular "I"

---

[5] Although Timothy is with Paul at the writing of 1 Corinthians, 2 Corinthians, and Colossians.

and the first person plural "we." The fact is that "we" tends to be used in 2 Corinthians when referring to the ministry team, thus "the hardships 'we' suffered" (1:3–12; 7:5–6); "our competence" comes from God (3:1–18); "Make room for us in your hearts. We have wronged no one" (7:2; 10:3–7; 11:12); "we are not trying to commend ourselves" (5:12). Though 1:13 may read "We write you what you can read and understand," suggesting multiple authorship, 13:6 states, "I trust that you will discover that we have not failed." Further, the travel plans and directions for action tend to be in the first person singular (e.g., 2:1–13; 9:1–5). All of this taken together draws one to the conclusion that the perspective and the language in which it is expressed is Paul's, but he writes with his coworkers in mind.

B. The Readers (1:1b–2)

In a similar manner to the way Paul approaches dual authorship, moving back and forth between the singular "I" and the plural "we" to represent himself as author with or without his colleagues' inclusion, so does he address both the Corinthians in particular and the Achaians in general: "To the church of God in Corinth, together with all the saints throughout Achaia" (2 Cor. 1:1). Paul had planned to visit Corinth (2 Cor. 1:23) and he exhorts the Corinthians specifically (e.g., "We have spoken freely to you, Corinthians" [2 Cor. 6:11]), but in regard to financial giving in chapters 8–9 his letter is addressed generally, comparing the generosity of the residents of the region of Macedonia with that of the inhabitants of Achaia (2 Cor. 9:2; 1:1).

1. The Saints Throughout Achaia (1:1b).

The land of Achaia was mentioned as early as Homer's great Trojan war epic *The Iliad*, but Achaia's league of cities' disastrous decision to defy Rome rather than ally itself with her plunged it under Roman domination. Hence, it languished for over one hundred years. In 27 B.C. Augustus reorganized the empire, making subjected Achaia a senatorial province under a proconsul who resided in Corinth. In A.D. 15 Tiberius combined Achaia with Macedonia and Moesia, creating a vast imperial province governed by a legate based in Moesia, but Claudius disbanded this arrangement in A.D. 44, making Achaia and Macedonia again separate provinces. Thus, when Paul came to Achaia, he found Corinth once more the capital and government center of the province. Somewhere about the time of Paul's death in A.D. 66–67 Nero would finally give Achaia its freedom, though his successor Vespasian would again place it under domination as a senatorial province. This jockeying back and forth of Achaia's status shows how desirable and powerful the province and its cities were. Corinth, as its chief city, thrived for ten more years until a massive earthquake shattered the city in A.D. 77.

Paul's sage advice was soberly demonstrated: to be generous, for wealth was only temporary; and want, though unobserved, could be very near. Throughout history the remnants of Corinth have been plagued by earthquakes. One of the most severe earthquakes in Greek history devastated the city in A.D. 375. By the mid-sixth century a series of wars and earthquakes had nearly depopulated Corinth. After the earthquake of 1858, the frustrated population abandoned the ancient site and moved the modern city some four miles (17 km.) away to a safer spot on the coast. That decision was soon supported when yet another major earthquake struck in 1928. Today old Corinth is in ruins. Only a little village *Palia Corinthos*, like a custodian, caretakes the crumbling masonry that once was mighty Corinth. How little the frivolous Corinthians foresaw their fate as they fawned over the superapostles and flippantly flirted with immorality and ungodly extravagance!

2. Paul's Relationship with the Achaians (1:1b).

According to the book of Acts, Paul did not visit Corinth until the second missionary journey. Paul, we remember, arrived in Corinth alone. Some of the Jews from Thessalonica had followed Paul, Silas, and Timothy to Berea, inciting the crowds, so the Christians sent Paul ahead to Athens to protect him. Paul entreated Silas and Timothy to join him as soon as possible.

Meanwhile, Acts 18:2 tells us that about A.D. 49, the Roman emperor Claudius had issued a decree against Jewish Christians, and as a result Aquila and Priscilla had "recently" come from Italy to Corinth. What a powerful team these three Christian tentmakers made when they came together, creating an interdependent economic and evangelistic community business/ministry. When Silas and Timothy arrived from Macedonia, Paul could preach full-time, stirring up the city with the startling message of Jesus (Acts 18:5ff.). Paul worked and preached for a year and six months while Lucius Junius Gallio was proconsul of the province of Achaia. Finally, the enraged Jews dragged Paul before Gallio. From an inscription about Gallio discovered at Delphi, we surmise this was probably in the summer of A.D. 51. Paul then was in Corinth from 50–51, working, preaching, and writing 1 and 2 Thessalonians. Acts 18:18 tells us he stayed many days longer after his aborted trial; scholars speculate that it was about three months more. Sometime between late autumn 51 and early 52 he left Corinth, returning to Antioch, while Aquila and Priscilla remained at Ephesus.

Paul set out on his third missionary journey, visiting the region of Galatia (to whose believers he had written Galatians) and Phrygia (the eventual site of one of the greatest of the earliest heresy controversies, Montanism [Acts 18:23]). About the same time, the great preacher Apollos traveled to Achaia and within it to Corinth, carrying a letter of introduction (Acts 18:27–19:1). Meanwhile, Paul was investing nearly three years preaching in Asia, using Ephesus as his base. Ephesus, later the base of the apostle John, had now become Paul's "home church." Resolving to go to Macedonia, Achaia, Jerusalem, and finally Rome, Paul sent two of his team, Timothy and Erastus, on ahead to Macedonia into Corinth (Acts 19:21–22; 1 Cor. 4:17; 16:10) and received news of Corinth (1 Cor. 1:11; 16:17; 7:1). First Corinthians is written in Ephesus (16:8, 19) in the spring, ca. 56. Second Corinthians 2:1 tells us Paul traveled to Corinth (the "painful visit") and returned to Ephesus sometime during this period, ca. 56. (Might this be when the "epistle of tears" was carried by Titus, who was sent to restore order and begin the collection process [2:9, 13; 7:6–12; 8:6]?)

After the merchants in Ephesus flung themselves into an uproar over Paul's competitive teaching to the worship of Artemis, Paul sought Titus in Macedonia via Troas. He learned that Titus had some success with the Corinthians. Paul traveled a third time to Corinth while spending three months in Greece, leaving from Philippi to return to Asia (Acts 20:2–3; 2 Cor. 12:14; 13:1–2). To speed up his journey he traveled past Ephesus by ship, wanting to be in Jerusalem by Pentecost (Acts 20:16). In Jerusalem, James, Jesus' brother, and the elders notified Paul that thousands of Jews in Jerusalem had believed, but they were antagonistic to Paul because he taught "apostasy from Moses" (that is, downplaying circumcision and the ritual customs [Acts 21:18–21]).

What a dramatic shift this accusation illustrated in the former "Pharisee of Pharisees" Saul. Indeed, the Jews from Asia did incite the crowd and had Paul arrested for advocating "Jews becoming Gentiles." To avoid an ambush, ca. A.D. 57, Paul was dispatched to Caesarea where he stayed over two years (Acts 24:27). Paul's troubles continued and, relying on his Roman citizenship once again, he appealed to the emperor, and was sent as prisoner to Rome ca. A.D. 59. Paul lived for at least two years under guard in Rome (Acts 28:16, 30). Some early traditions suggest that Paul was released, ca. 61–62, before he returned a second time to Rome to be martyred during the latter part of Nero's reign (ca. 64–68). Eusebius, the great church historian from the early 300s wrote, "It is recorded that in [Nero's] reign Paul was beheaded in Rome" (*History of the Church* 2.25).

When—in this period of uproarious turmoil, deep ministering relationships, shipwrecks, scourgings, delightful Christian celebrations, fervent prayer vigils, narrow escapes, happy festivities, dogged persecution, famine, plenty, joy, and eventual martyrdom—did Paul find time to write the Corinthians not one but several letters? To determine the date of a letter, we must first find its place of dispatch. Second Corinthians 13:1 tells us the letter was written before Paul's third visit to Corinth. Acts only records two visits to Corinth, but his third visit would probably be part of the brief visit to Greece recorded in Acts 20:2, his final recorded visit before his lengthy imprisonment. We know that 2 Corinthians alludes to many of his adventures, revealing that it follows them and must be written toward the end of his ministry. Second Corinthians 11:32, which corresponds with Acts 9:19–25, tells of his escape from Aretas at

Damascus early in his ministry. Second Corinthians 12:2 refers to a revelation fourteen years earlier, and 1:8, 16; 2:12; 7:5 mention Asia, Macedonia, and Troas (places we have just seen) that he visited both on his second and third missionary journeys.

In the account of his personal travels, Paul mentions he completed his journey to Macedonia (2 Cor. 7:5), and in 9:2 he employs the present tense, "For I know your eagerness to help, and I am boasting about it to the Macedonians." In 9:4 he uses the subjunctive (the mood that means—"maybe it will happen") to describe the possibility that some Macedonians may accompany him to help him receive Achaia's donation to aid famine-stricken Christians in Israel. If we corroborate this scriptural data with such archaeological data as the Gallio inscription we cited earlier (that established Paul's stay in Corinth to end about A.D. 52), and if we take into account the nearly three years spent in Ephesus and environs with a second visit to Corinth (ca. 56), 2 Corinthians was most likely written about 56 to 57 from somewhere in Macedonia after Paul received the Macedonian offerings (2 Cor. 8:1–5). He then sent Titus and some others ahead with the letter (2 Cor. 8:6, 16–24), for Corinth had not yet made its donation (2 Cor. 8:7, 11). Very soon afterwards, as we have seen, Paul would be arrested in Rome (ca. 57), beginning the long litigation that would end in release and rearrest, and eventually in Paul's receiving the same crown that so many years earlier he had watched bestowed upon Stephen—that of martyr for Christ.

3. The Church of God in Corinth (1:1b).

a. What was Corinth like? (1:1b) Imposing Corinth stood as the hub of a three-city complex, straddling the southwest end of the tiny isthmus that connects the southern part of the Greek peninsula to the mainland. About two miles north was Lechaeum with Cenchreae, home of Phoebe of Romans 16:1–2, lying over six miles east.

As far back as 4000 B.C. small settlements had been attracted by the springs and the massive rock mountain rising up to the sky, later called the Acrocorinth, which made an ideal fortress. Ephyra, meaning "lookout, guard," was Corinth's original name. Before 1800 B.C. those adventurous sailors, the Phoenicians,

were especially dominant, and brought their worship of Aphrodite to this strategic outpost. By 900 B.C. the Dorian cult of
Argive Hera had arrived, and Corinth was developing into a
naval and economic center. By the 400s B.C. it was regarded as
one of the three major powers in Greece along with Athens and
Sparta. Headstrong and arrogant, Corinth instigated the Pelo-
ponnesian War of 431–404 B.C., pitting Sparta against Athens,
which Sparta won with Persian aid. Then, aligning with Athens,
it overturned Sparta's rule, freeing the cities from Spartan
supremacy.

Now Corinth was drawn into its most ambitious project:
aligning with the Achaean League. The League, comprised of
eleven Greek city states, had united in war against King Philip
II of Macedon. But Philip defeated the League in 338 B.C. and
set up a garrison in the great fortress hill, the Acrocorinth. The
war may have gone in Philip's favor but the political scheming
was far from over, and Philip was assassinated in 336. Aratos,
general of the Achaean League, seized the fortress on the
Acrocorinth in 243 B.C. and strategically handed it over to
Corinth, who responded by joining the Achaean League. Now
Corinth's ambition came to the fore, and by 150 B.C. it had
become the capital of the League.

Led by Corinth, the league rejected a demand for dissolution by a Roman legation in 147 B.C., and marshaling its forces,
the League rose to pit itself against the new threat of world
domination sweeping out from the burgeoning city-state Rome.
Rome, though, was not an assimilating type of conqueror as
Philip and his son Alexander the Great had been. Swiftly and
terribly in one year Imperial Rome crushed the Achaean
League, and in fury the Roman forces led by consul Lucius
Mummius razed the city of Corinth in 146 B.C., burning it to the
ground, destroying it utterly. The ancients had praised the
beauty of Corinth, but by 130 B.C. Antipator of Sidon was
mourning, "Where is thy celebrated beauty, Doric Corinth? . . .
Not even a trace is left of thee, most unhappy of towns, but war
has seized on and devoured everything."[6] Everything devastat-

---

[6]*Greek Anthology* 9:151 cited by Jerome Murphy-O'Connor, *St. Paul's
Corinth: Texts and Archaeology*, Good News Studies 6 (Wilmington: Michael
Glazier, 1983), p. 44.

ed, its citizens sold into slavery, the ruins lay desolate for a century.

Then in 44 B.C., because of its strategic position, just days before his assassination, Julius Caesar decreed the refounding of Corinth as a military precaution. Renamed "Colonia Laus Julia Corinthiensis," the city had been rebuilt by a colony of Italian freedmen, Roman veterans, freed Greek slaves from Italy, other Greeks, Egyptian merchants, Phoenicians, Phrygians, Jews, and other Orientals. Latin had become its official language, and under Augustus Caesar, Julius Caesar's adopted son, it flourished.

In this mix a fully integrated church of Gentiles and Jews was planted. To the former Paul would write, "You know that when you were pagans, somehow or other you were influenced and led astray to mute idols" (1 Cor. 12:2). To the latter he soon counseled, "Was a man already circumcised when he was called? He should not become uncircumcised. Was a man uncircumcised when he was called? He should not be circumcised. Circumcision is nothing and uncircumcision is nothing. Keeping God's commands is what counts" (1 Cor. 7:18–19). This brand-new city lacked an aristocracy. Money and power (such as Strabo tells us those rich tyrants the Bacchiadae family and Cypselus wielded) became the rule of the day (Geography 8.6.20). Through Corinth money and power surged and, in less than twenty years of its refounding, Corinth became the capital of the province of Achaia and the administrative seat of the Roman government's proconsul for southern and central Greece. Thus, by the time Paul arrived in mighty Corinth, that capital and governmental center of Achaia had grown to a one-half-million-plus people in the barely one hundred years since its refounding.

What made Corinth prosper so? The southern tip of Greece around the horn of Cape Maleae was extremely dangerous. In fact, it was the most dangerous cape in the entire Mediterranean. Proverbs about it abounded as, "Let him who sails around Maleae first make his will," and "When you double Maleae, forget your home." Thus, almost all trade and travel from the east to the west had to be done through Corinth. Shipowners would sail their cargoes to the isthmus, and then at the narrowest point unload and haul them across the land to other ships waiting on the other side. If a ship were light enough, it was hauled the three-and-a-half miles on moveable trolleys. Corinth was situated on an elevated, breezy terrace, according to John Chrysostom (Discourses 6:3), two miles inland, guarding this narrow passageway. Controlling two ports—Lechaeum on the Gulf of Corinth (port to Rome) to the Ionian Sea and Cenchreae on the Saronic Gulf (port to East) to the Aegean Sea, Corinth collected the imperial duties, becoming a major banking and commercial center. Called the "Market-Place of Greece" by the second century A.D., it was Greece's finest city. Strabo wrote:

> Corinth is called "wealthy" because of its commerce, since it is situated on the Isthmus and is master of two harbors, of which the one leads straight to Asia, and the other to Italy; and it makes easy the exchange of merchandise from both countries that are so far distant from each other (Geography 8.6.20).

Corinth, however, was not just a banker or merchant. Corinth's crafts were renowned. Its pottery was beautiful, its bronze world-famous. Sextus Propertius, ca. 16, extolled its bronzes in his Elegies 3.5.3-6, while Strabo wrote:

> The city of the Corinthians, then, was always great and wealthy, and it was well equipped with men skilled both in the affairs of state and in the craftsman's arts; for both here and in Sicyon the arts of painting and modeling and all such arts of the craftsman flourished most (Geography 8.6.23).

Further, the Isthmian games, second only to the Olympics, were celebrated every two years and went back under Corinth's control sometime between 7 B.C. and A.D. 3, so the profits flowed in.

b. What were the Corinthians like? (1:1b–2) Corinth boasted of its intellectual activity, but it paled beside Athens and Alexandria and could not hold as resident a single person of letters. The church at Corinth, too, loved prophecy and knowledge, preferring speech over love (1 Cor. 1:5; 6:12; 11:13; 13:8–9; 14:2; 2 Cor. 8:7), but like the city, it pursued knowledge avidly but not wisely. Paul notes in 1 Corinthians 1:5 that, "in every way you were enriched in [Christ Jesus] with all speech and all knowledge" (RSV), but he cautions in 13:8–9: "But where there are prophecies, they will cease; where there are tongues, they will be stilled; where there is knowledge, it will pass away." "Love," he teaches the Corinthians, "never fails." And again in 2 Corinthians 8:7 he urges, "But just as you excel in everything—in faith, in speech, in knowledge, in complete earnestness and in your love for us—see that you also excel in this grace of giving."

Corinth was a town of the nouveau riche, it had no real roots. What Paul alludes to in the Corinthian church was true of the city as well: "Your abundance at the present time ... " (2 Cor. 8:14 RSV). This sudden influx of wealth in a rootless boomtown made Corinth like one vast drunken sailor, all at once rich with pay, squandering its swiftly gotten gains on pleasure and dissolution. And, indeed, Corinth was the most immoral city in Greece, perhaps in the entire Roman empire. Its prostitutes were legion and many of these, as we shall see, were tied into the chief religion, a faith totally dissolute. Paul warns the church in 1 Corinthians 6:9–11 that the male prostitutes, idolators, adulterers, homosexuals, sensualists (*malakos*—the soft or effete—transvestites?), drunks, and thieves that made up a good deal of Corinth's population were not going to inherit the kingdom of God.

As early as the days of the redoubtable satirist Aristophanes (about 450–385 B.C.) Corinth had been working on its immoral reputation. He coined the verb *Corinthiadzomai* (to live like a Corinthian) to mean: to practice fornication. A *Corinthiastes* was a whoremonger, and a "Corinthian girl" a prostitute. A Corinthian on the stage was always presented as drunk, and even in recent times, the term "Corinthians" was applied to wealthy young men who lived in reckless and riotous carousing, drunk and immoral. Essentially, Corinth was a pit full of money, power, immorality, and dissolution, infamous for its riotous luxury and extravagance. It had the dissolution of New York's 42nd Street with the wealth of Beverly Hills.

What kind of people would be produced by such a city? Paul reminds the church of Corinth of what they, too, had been: sexually immoral, drunken thieves, steeped in idol worship. "And that is what some of you were," he lectures, "But you were

washed, you were sanctified, you were justified in the name of
the Lord Jesus Christ and by the Spirit of our God" (1 Cor.
6:11). Residual sins such as the problems with incest in
1 Corinthians 5 and the need to marry "since there is so much
immorality" in 7:2 had to be brought to attention and eradicated
in the Corinthian church. Paul realized the task was a monu-
mental one. He is firm with them throughout his correspondence, but understanding of their frailties. He may become
exasperated with their stupidity and cupidity, but he does not
give up on them. He sees what generous, upright citizens of
God's reign they can become. And he does not forget that
personal and cultural history is an immense mountain out of
which he must dig the ore of the Corinthians' God-created
selves. Four hundred years earlier Diogenes, probable founder
of the Cynics, was said to have come to Corinth because he
thought even then that they needed to hear his message of social
protest and ascetic frugality. Paul knew that such a long history
of waywardness could not be straightened out overnight. But the
grace of God begins a lifelong work that the Holy Spirit brings
slowly to completion, and Paul wanted to guide the Corinthians
on that holy way to the mansions prepared for them by Jesus.

Still, living in Corinth had ill-prepared the Corinthians for
taking up the responsibilities of citizenship in God's reign. In
almost every letter of Paul to a congregation, the apostle begins
with a similar sentence: "I (or 'we') give thanks (*eucharistō* or
one of its derivatives) to God," often assuring the recipients that
his prayers are with them, as in Ephesians 1:16 and Philemon 4.
Thus he opens 1 Thessalonians 1:2–3; 2 Thessalonians 1:3;
Romans 1:8; Philippians 1:3–6; Colossians 1:3; even 1 Corinthians 1:4. Then he follows this sentence by listing the positive
qualities he appreciates in each congregation. He thanks God
for the Thessalonians' faith, love, and steadfastness; Philemon's
and the Colossians' and Ephesians' faith and love; the Romans'
faith; the Philippians' "partnership in the gospel"; and initially,
in 1 Corinthians, Paul thanked God for the grace that enriched
the Corinthians in speech and knowledge. We soon see in
studying each letter that what is included or omitted in Paul's
opening address is very significant. It is a clue to Paul's
evaluation of each congregation's spiritual progress. Second

Corinthians and Galatians are the only letters in which Paul does not express any thanks to God for any congregational virtue.

In 2 Corinthians, Paul instead plunges immediately into a discussion of his suffering. The only thanks he mentions is in 1:11 and that is only potential, for he begs the Corinthians to help him and his associates by prayer so that others will give thanks on their behalf. Paul has nothing to be thankful about in the present condition of the Corinthians. Like the Galatians, they had deserted his leadership. The Corinthians were a cantankerous, rebellious lot. They were tempted to fall back into their past lives, and the Gentiles among them were still within easy reach of idolatry.

Beautiful Corinth was laid out in such a way that pagan temples were literally everywhere. Towering over the city, perched on the sheer cliffs of the gray limestone of the Acrocorinth, reclined one of Corinth's temples of Aphrodite, goddess of love. More than one thousand temple slaves or prostitutes served the great sanctified brothel of Aphrodite, and though the number may have fallen off by the time Paul visited, dissolution and decadence still characterized its religious rites. Further, a winding road up the mountain to the fortress passed shrine after shrine to Demeter, to the Great Mother, to Isis, to Serapis, and so on. Along the road to Sicyon stood the Temple of Asclepius, where people went to be healed, leaving crafted images of ears and feet showing health restored by the god. Down in the city proper, temples ringed the marketplace: the imposing Temple of Apollo, the temple of Tyche, the temple of Hermes, another temple to Aphrodite, a temple to the Pantheon—the many gods.

If Paul and Aquila and Priscilla had their store in the older northwest shops, they would have worked right across the street from the shrines. Or more likely, if their business was in the newly opened shop area on the Lechaeum Road, they would have been in the shadow of Apollo's sanctuary near the smaller meatmarket. The wise shopper found bargains in these meats offered to idols, sold at reduced rates. Many temples had dining facilities—they were, in effect, the ancient equivalent of clubs: the Rotary, Moose, Elks, Kiwanis of the pagans. A popular game was *kottabos*, a sort of first century food fight, where one guest held up his cup as a target for another guest to hit with wine flicked from his cup. Dionysus, the wine god, was a popular deity to worship, or one could visit the temples of Athena Chalinitis, Hera Akraia, or Octavia—rest at the statue of Poseidon, or church hunt at numerous small temples along the west wing of the marketplace. With social life, grocery buying, and a good deal of commerce all tied into idolatry, swimming against the flow for the flabby consciences of the Corinthians was extremely strenuous, many going under, some (like the incestuous man of 1 Corinthians 5) for perhaps the last time.

The Jews of the congregation, whose synagogue was also on the Lechaeum Road, fared somewhat better as far as idolatry and immorality were concerned. Initially, the Jews of Corinth had resisted Paul, becoming abusive (as Acts 18:6 tells us). But Crispus, the synagogue ruler, and his entire household believed. Acts 18:17 tells us that when the enraged synagogue members dragged Paul before proconsul Gallio, who summarily rejected their suit and tossed them out of court, they turned on Sosthenes, the synagogue ruler, and beat him in front of the court. Did Paul minister to the battered Sosthenes? Did he give him his arm and help him limp to the home of Titius Justus or Crispus, or did he take him to Priscilla and Aquila where together they patched him up, body and spirit? Whether Sosthenes was abandoned by his fellows for failing to have Paul indicted or whether he had allowed Paul to speak in the synagogue, therefore being blamed for not stopping him, we are not certain. But we do see Paul ministering in Ephesus, where 1 Corinthians was written, with a Christian Sosthenes who may well have been this very same beaten synagogue ruler (1 Cor. 1:1). At any rate, the Jews who joined the church were a more righteous and faithful lot.

But whether more-moral Jew or lax Gentile, the Corinthians had one vice in general. They were stingy. Compared to other churches, the Corinthians at that time had financial abundance (2 Cor. 8:14), but Paul did not consider many of them to be wise, powerful, or noble (1 Cor. 1:26). The Crispuses in the congregation who had ruled synagogues were few, and it seemed the ignoble Corinthians were more likely to flaunt their newly gained wealth than share it (1 Cor. 11:21–22).

Like most miserly people, they wanted their preachers, Barnabas and Paul, to earn their own living and to minister gratis (1 Cor. 9:6–18). Yet when Paul received financial support from Macedonia, the Corinthians became jealous and suspicious that somehow Paul was taking advantage of them (2 Cor. 7:2)! Though he had the right, Paul did not charge the Corinthians for his services to them (2 Cor. 11:7–9), scrupulously avoiding the accusation of being a "peddler" of God's word.

At times the Corinthians could be loyal to Paul (1 Cor. 11:2; 2 Cor. 7:15), maintaining his teachings. They did have a zeal for Paul and were grieved by his letter, wanting his approval (2 Cor. 2:4), but they were fickle and unreliable. Paul was not certain of their total obedience (2 Cor. 2:9). The doubt he had about their truly fulfilling their financial obligations was an indication of their irresponsibility, and their lack of loyalty toward Paul (2 Cor. 8:7; 9:1–5). To Paul they were children in Christ (1 Cor. 3:1; 2 Cor. 6:13), still questioning such foundational doctrines as the resurrection of the dead (1 Cor. 15:12). Like all of Corinth, they made a great pretense of wisdom, preferring prophecy, knowledge, freedom of thought and speech over love. As a result they lorded it over one another and fell out in disputes with each other, taking each other to court (1 Cor. 1:10; 6:1; 11:18; 2 Cor. 13:1, 11).

In their flightiness they managed to be both immoral (1 Cor. 5:1–11; 6:9–18; 2 Cor. 12:21) and ascetic (1 Cor. 7:1; 2 Cor. 2:6–7), moderation being the only commodity scarce in Corinth. They were sometimes autocratic (2 Cor. 2:6–7) and arrogant (1 Cor. 4:18–19). They were characterized by strife, jealousy, anger, disputing, slander, gossip, conceit, and disorder (2 Cor. 12:20), and were boastful and judgmental (1 Cor. 4:3, 7, 10; 5:6). They criticized Paul's personal appearance, his presence, and his speech, snidely contrasting his speaking ability with the God-inspired power of his writing (2 Cor. 10:10; 11:6). They fawned over eloquent speakers with their apostate gospels (2 Cor. 11:4, 19; 13:5), demanding proof that Christ was truly speaking through the unimpressive Paul (2 Cor. 11:6; 13:3).

Even if the ancient world had had the know-how, a TV ministry by Paul would have floundered in Corinth.

Essentially, the Corinthian church was made up of Gentile enthusiasts, swept away by their emotions to every golden-tongued orator. They were suspiciously distrustful, yet easy to deceive; unreliable, not to be trusted to fulfill their promises; sometimes arrogant and autocratic yet obsequious; hedonistic yet ascetic at turns; frivolous and changeable in their loyalty to Paul; easily influenced by impressive, autocratic leaders. What a loathsome and disappointing bunch of losers the Corinthians appear to have been! How human in their failings, so much like all of us in our worst and weakest moments. That God could love the Corinthians, and Paul could persevere despite continual disappointments to love and serve them, is such a comforting word to us all. For Paul assured the errant Corinthians again and again that he loved them (2 Cor. 2:2–4; 7:3; 11:11; 12:15; 13:10). Incredible as such a thought may seem, he can take pride in them and they can give him joy (1 Cor. 4:15; 2 Cor. 7:3–16; 9:2). How can he overlook the incontrovertible fact that they are easy prey for any arrogant, strutting, false apostle? That by any view they are a wealthy, moral slum?

He can forgive all their failings because he regards them as a father does a child. Indeed, he is their spiritual father (Acts 18:1–18; 2 Cor. 11:2; 12:14; 10:14), and because of this parental love he can be hurt by the loss of their devotion, wounded by their harsh criticism (2 Cor. 10:1; 11:5). Vulnerable to them, Paul wants their commendation for all his struggle and suffering on their behalf (2 Cor. 3:1; 12:11), and he dreads the inevitable disappointment both he and the Corinthians will experience in one another when they meet (2 Cor. 12:20–21). He is deeply disturbed about their faith (2 Cor. 11:1–3; 13:5), suspecting that in turning from him they are also turning from the true gospel of Jesus Christ. He implores them urgently, "Follow my example, as I follow the example of Christ" (1 Cor. 11:1). This exhortation will be a foundational plea lying beneath the passion, the disappointment, the disapproval, and the imploring exhortation to pure devotion, sincere motives, and right actions that will comprise the poignant entreaty that is 2 Corinthians.

For Further Study

1. Using a Study Bible map, follow Paul's travels as you read the Book of Acts.

2. Use an unabridged concordance to discover the importance of tents, tentmakers, and tabernacles in the Bible.

3. Use a concordance to gather positive and negative traits and exemplary and nonexemplary examples of Pharisees in the New Testament.

4. Who were Paul's coworkers? Use the word lexicon in Young's, Strong's, or Englishman's *Greek Concordance* to find all references to *sunergos*. What was unique about each coworker?

5. Read 1 and 2 Corinthians, collating the positive and negative spiritual qualities of the Corinthian church. What are the positive and negative spiritual qualities of your own church? What qualities do you have that are similar to those of the Corinthians?

Chapter 2

Paul's Defense: We Behave Sincerely with Pure Motives in God's Grace
(2 Corinthians 1:3–2:17)

Paul does not explicitly say, "Well, I am going to defend my style of leadership, and here's the first reason." If he had, the Corinthians would never have listened to him. Paul faces the dilemma of defending the truth that he received from God about what comprises a genuine servant of God, without appearing defensive. Here, certainly, we find Paul caught between the immovable object and the irresistible force. Paul wanted first to explain how someone without a pure motive would never experience the afflictions that he, Timothy, and the others experienced. Second, he wanted to explain that his change of plans to visit the Corinthians in the past was not due to his own fickleness but, rather, to his concern to spare the Corinthians a painful visit. So, Paul begins elaborating what he has learned about "God our Father and the Lord Jesus Christ" (1:2).

A. Paul's Team Experiences Afflictions in Asia (1:3–11)

Certainly this passage is one of the most moving and poignant passages ever written. Paul interweaves an explanation of God's nature with an accounting of the difficulties that the Christians had been currently experiencing, into a fabric that glorifies God while it sympathizes with human pathos. In these verses is an implicit description of what Paul will slowly unpack throughout the letter.

1. Praising God in the midst of afflictions (1:3–7).

Paul begins, as would have many a devout Jew, praising God. How is God here described? God is the "Father" (which

45

here is a metaphor for "Creator," the source) of "compassion" (NIV) or "mercies" (RSV) and the God of all "comfort." "Compassion" and "comfort" are highlighted in this paragraph.

"Compassion" is a poetical word. The Greek word (*oiktirmos*) contains within it the root word for "pity" and "oh!" (*oi*). The verb means "to pity" or "to have compassion on (someone)."[1] Many of the ancients considered the viscera or bowels to be the seat of compassion, even as now we may describe "gut-level feelings" to indicate deeply felt emotions. "Compassion" rarely occurs in the New Testament, but when Paul uses it, he uses it significantly.

When Paul builds up to his appeal to the Romans to present their bodies as a living sacrifice (12:1), the basis for his appeal is the "mercy" of God. When he makes his appeal to the Philippians (2:1) that they "complete" his joy by being of the same mind, again he includes the word "compassion" as the basis for their action. James also cites God's "compassion" as a reason for oppressed Christians to be patient and steadfast. God will have compassion on the oppressed (by punishing the wicked!) (James 5:11).

"Compassion" is a characteristic of God. Therefore we, too, must follow God's example. In 3:12 Paul tells the Colossians to "put on" "compassion," literally "compassion of compassion," the first trait preceding kindness, humility, gentleness, and patience. As Jesus said, we must "be merciful, just as our Parent [in heaven] is merciful" (Luke 6:36).

Paul does not, in 2 Corinthians, state that God's compassion *must* be the basis for their repentance, because at this time the Corinthians were not believing much in a God of mercy. However, Paul states what, in fact, is the basis of his own work and should be the basis of the work of all Christians—God's great mercy.

That God is compassionate is emphasized by the next phrase because it is a synonym, "God of all comfort." The word

---

[1]The definitions used in this commentary are quoted from H. G. Liddell and Robert Scott, *A Greek-English Lexicon* 9th ed. (Oxford: Clarendon, 1940); Walter Bauer, *A Greek-English Lexicon of the New Testament* (Chicago: University, 1957); Joseph Henry Thayer, *Thayer's Greek-English Lexicon of the New Testament* (Marshallton: National Foundation for Christian Education, 1885); or, our own study of the New Testament.

family "comfort," from which we get our word "paraklete" (one name for the Holy Spirit), occurs ten times in 1:3–7. Certainly Paul is trying to hit his readers with a thought.

"Comfort" has a more action-oriented sense in the Greek language than it usually has in English. "I comfort" means "I call for," "I call to my side, summon, appeal" as one summons one's friends as witnesses in a trial. As Jesus says when he is arrested, he could if he wanted, "appeal" to his Father, and God at once would send more than twelve legions of angels to defend him (Matt. 26:53). God "comforts" us by being the Friend who will testify on our behalf at our trial. Our God is not only a God who soothes our feelings, but our God is also the one who acts to grant us vindication, to pronounce us "not guilty."

Paul begins by describing God, and then goes on to elaborate how God's nature affected Paul and his associates, and through them had an impact on the Corinthians themselves. Like the rain that flows down the mountain to form rivers and lakes and waterfalls, so God's "comfort" affects humans who then go on to affect other humans.

Who is the "God of all comfort"? That God is the one who not just once but continually stands at our side defending us and helping us as we get buffeted by the trouble-bringing prosecutor (1:4). "Troubles" or "afflictions" (*thlipsis*) literally refers to "pressure" or "crushing." The sensation of something pressing down on something else (as feet on grapes) is akin to people external to ourselves discriminating ("oppression") or causing some other difficulty ("affliction"). For example, Jesus had to preach from a boat so that the crowd would not "crowd" or "crush" him (Mark 3:9). Usually the metaphor refers to external difficulties such as famine, slavery, persecution, and imprisonment (Acts 7:10–11; 11:19; 20:23; Eph. 3:13). Jesus certainly warned his followers that these types of difficulties were sure to come. People who are well rooted in their confidence in God will be able to withstand them (Matt. 13:21; 24:9; John 16:33; 2 Thess. 1:4). The way is "hard" that leads to life (Matt. 7:14).

In 2 Corinthians 1:4 we learn that as God's word becomes actualized and we find that we are in the midst of difficulties, God will be there helping us. The result will be that we, in turn, will be made able to help others who are experiencing difficulties. If Jesus taught his followers to be merciful as God is merciful, Paul here explains that one can be merciful or help another because one has already received mercy or been helped by God. Not only must we "do to others what we would have them do to us" (Matt. 7:12), but also we *can* "do to others" *because* others "have done to us." Often we hear about parents who treat their children roughly and their children inadvertently go on to do the same with their own children. However, we need to notice the reverse: that those who receive compassion themselves go on to give compassion.

The difficulties that Paul mentions are ones that come *not* from sin but from living a Christian life, because they are "the sufferings of Christ" (2 Cor. 1:5). Paul compares the abundance of suffering with the abundance of comfort. If one increases, so does the other.

"Comfort" is not simply a vertical matter between God and one human. It is also horizontal, between one human and another. Paul tells the Corinthians that he is willing to suffer for their well-being. He also is comforted for their well-being. We shall see later that Paul's opponents at Corinth do not agree with this philosophy. Paul, in effect, writes of a partnership. If believers are partners in suffering, they will also be partners in comfort (2 Cor. 1:7). The implication that has not yet been developed is that the comfort will not come without the suffering.

2. The nature of their afflictions (1:8–11).

Paul has not been writing in the abstract as the religious person who places a heavy burden on another without "lifting one finger" to help (Luke 11:46; Matt. 23:4). He speaks in the plural of the experiences of himself and his associates.

We learn that Paul does not stoically accept his sufferings. Neither does he see them as good in themselves. If never sharing one's troubles were a Christian virtue, Paul would have no virtue at all. This type of fatalism is not part of Christianity but a leftover of ancient astrology where the stars controlled one's life apart from one's actions. Instead, Paul declares that the troubles they experienced in Asia were "far beyond their abilities to endure."

What troubles could Paul be speaking of? He describes them as being so severe that he and his associates doubted they would live. They felt as if they had received "the sentence of death" from a jury (2 Cor. 1:9). These hardships probably occurred after 1 Corinthians was written, since the Corinthians had been uninformed about them (2 Cor. 1:8).

First Corinthians was written from Ephesus where "there were many who opposed" Paul (1 Cor. 16:9). If Timothy also experienced these hardships ("wild beasts in Ephesus," 1 Cor. 15:32), then Paul is describing events in Asia that occurred between Acts 18:23 and 19:22. Luke's only clue to these troubles occurs in Acts 19:9, where some of the Jews at the synagogue "became obstinate; they refused to believe and publicly maligned the Way." If Timothy were not included, the hardships would include those received from Gentiles as well, as when Paul, Gaius, Aristarchus, and others were attacked by an angry mob (Acts 19:23–40). Gaius and Aristarchus were brought to the forum in Ephesus by a rioting crowd. Probably this one incident was recorded by Luke simply as an illustration of the difficulties Paul and his associates endured, in this case, for undermining the religious and economic well-being of a city. Luke understates that Artemis "brought in no little business" to the merchants (Acts 19:24) to accentuate the positive: it was the major business enterprise at Ephesus. (The temple of Artemis was one of the seven wonders of the ancient world.) Paul will go on to specify exactly what troubles he endured later in 2 Corinthians (e.g., 11:23–33).

Nowhere in this passage does Paul say that any of these troubles come from God. If that were true, Paul would then be praying for difficulties. Masochism, which seeks suffering, should never be a part of the Christian life. Rather, although Paul in this chapter assumes that hardships will be part of the life of any genuine Christian, God is never said to cause them. God, though, can deliver us from any affliction, and in the process, as Paul did, we can learn that God is indeed compassionate, helpful, and powerful enough to raise us up from out of our troubles. God is not only the One who always is in the process of helping us (2 Cor. 1:4), but God is also the One who always is in the process of raising the dead (2 Cor. 1:9). No death or no trouble is too great for God. Paul has confidence that God was the One who rescued him, and God will be the One who will rescue him in the future.

Paul speaks of a community of suffering and comfort; he concludes with a community of thanksgiving. Trouble, comfort, and thanksgiving all stand together. Even as Jesus appreciated the one healed leper who thanked him (Luke 17:11–19), so, too, God in heaven appreciates our thanks. Paul sees that believers can cooperate with the prayers of other believers. If the Corinthians were to pray, giving thanks for the deliverance of Paul and his associates, they would then, in effect, feel that they had been presented with a gift (2 Cor. 1:11). Paul is saying that he would be pleased if the Corinthians thanked God for the happy ending to these difficulties. This type of caring and sharing community is the type of community that belongs to a caring and sharing God.

B. Paul's Planning Was Sincere (1:12–2:17)

In the first eleven verses of chapter one, Paul has been showing that persons without pure motives would not experience severe afflictions. To spare the Corinthians another painful visit, from 1:12 through 2:17 he writes about his change of plans, explaining that they were not due to vacillation but to love.

1. The Main Point of the Letter (1:12–2:2).

No direct word of defense has been said by Paul until 1:12. This sentence is the key not only to this section of the letter, but also to the entire letter. In effect, it is Paul's thesis statement.

Paul uses "boast" or "boasting" or "object of boasting" at least twenty-eight times in this one letter. Some readers have taken the term literally—Paul is indeed "boasting," as *Webster's Dictionary* defines it, speaking with "pride, vanity, or exultation"; bragging about. The Greek lexicon also defines "boasting" as "speaking loud" or "vaunting oneself," or praising or glorying (on account) of a thing or person. How can Paul "boast," when for many people the greatest sin is pride?

First, we often confuse self-effacement and modesty with humility. A self-effacing person is one who will never accept compliments or public praise. "Mary, your sermon was well-

prepared, well-organized, and well-delivered!" If Mary were
self-effacing, she would say, "Oh, it was nothing." Is that really
lack of pride? Genuine humility is to consider one's needs and
value as no less but no more important than anyone else's needs
and value. As Paul says, "we are coworkers" (2 Cor. 1:24) or
"servants of Christ" (1 Cor. 4:1). Therefore, "boasting," if it
simply means "praising" when it is truthful, is by no means a
sin. Rather, we are required to praise and glorify one another
(1 Cor. 12:26). To speak honestly about ourselves is simply a
cultural practice that varies from one culture to another.
Therefore, Paul does not speak with undue vanity when he says
that he can honestly say that he and his associates have
conducted themselves with pure motives with the Corinthians.

Second, Paul uses several key terms in 2 Corinthians which
were either being used by the Corinthians to attack Paul, or
which, in reality, described the *Corinthians* themselves rather
than Paul or his coworkers. Paul will explicitly say in 2 Corinthians 10:12–18 that some people at Corinth were boasting of
accomplishments achieved by another person (the implication
may be that they were taking credit for Paul's own work). They
were "boasting" dishonestly or deceitfully. Paul then says that
what counts is not what one says about oneself but what God
says about oneself. Therefore, Paul will always see his own
work and accomplishments as done within God's providence, as
he says in 1:12, "according to God's grace."

Verse 1:12 is an apt summary of 2 Corinthians. Paul's main
point is that he and his associates have conducted themselves
both in the world at large and certainly toward the Corinthians
with purity of motives in the grace of God. In contrast, they have
not conducted themselves "in fleshly wisdom" ("worldly wisdom" [NIV]; "earthly wisdom" [RSV]). What "fleshly wisdom"
looks like will be developed in stages throughout the letter. In
1:17 it is described as someone who does not keep his word. In
2:17 the person is called a "peddler" of God's word. The focus
in this section is what Paul *is*, not what he is *not*.

Paul describes his team's conduct as done in "holiness and
sincerity." These two nouns are an apt summary of all the
conduct of Paul's coworkers. In effect, these words are a
pleonasm in which two synonyms are joined together to

intensify an idea. For example, instead of saying, "I was very sincere," you might say, "I was sincere and genuine." Both sentences communicate a similar idea.

His team's conduct is, first of all, "holy, set apart to or by God." "Holiness" can also signify "pure motive." Paul and his coworkers were not only morally pure and set apart to do God's work, but they also had pure motives. The second word, "sincerity," even more so highlights the idea of "unmixed," "pure" as a metal (without alloy). Paul will use this same word again in 2:17 to close off this passage.

To what behavior does the "pure motives" refer? First, it refers to Paul's writing style (1:13–14). Paul's goal is to be understood when he writes to the churches. He does not intend to overwhelm them with rhetorically impressive but incomprehensible language. For instance, the first-century philosopher Dionysius of Halicarnassus condemns popular rhetoricians who would add color to their speeches by abandoning ordinary language for artificial rhythms and words:

> They used a plethora of metaphors, exaggerations and other forms of figurative language, and further confused the ordinary members of their audiences by using obscure and exotic words, and by resorting to unfamiliar figures of speech and other novel modes of expression" (Lysias 3).

Paul certainly uses figurative language, but always for the purpose of edification and communication. The implication here is that Paul intends that the Corinthians understand because he is an ambassador of the God who understands all people and who wants all to understand. Christianity is not a secret club. As Jesus taught, "There is nothing concealed that will not be disclosed, or hidden that will not be made known" (Luke 12:2). God is the God of clarity, not confusion.

Second, "pure motives" refers to Paul's promises. Paul's promises can be trusted. Paul had intended to visit the Corinthians as he traveled to and from Macedonia (1:15–16; 1 Cor. 16:5–7). Since Paul usually went to Macedonia from its northernmost port, to have traveled to Corinth first would have been an extra effort. Nevertheless, Paul had intended to do that extra traveling so that the Corinthians would better understand his teachings. He did not go to Macedonia. Some of the Corinthians then started to consider him as someone who vacillates, someone fickle, someone who could not be trusted, someone who might say, "Yes, yes" when he intended, "No, no." Such a person would not have pure motives.

Second Corinthians is a magnificent letter illustrating how one's beliefs are and must be manifested in one's actions. If Paul's promise could not be trusted, then Paul's God could not be trusted. Therefore, Paul quickly explains how his team's message is as truthful and reliable as its God. All of God's promises are "Yes" in Jesus Christ. If Paul had described God as the One comforting, and the One raising (1:4, 9), now he describes God as the One confirming or causing to "stand firm" (1:21).

Paul changed his plans because of his pure motives. His behavior was motivated by love for the Corinthians. The "Yes" in Paul was "Yes" to love the Corinthians with a genuine love that would always act to further their faith and joy. Because Paul loved the Corinthians, he was free to change his plans. As he mentions at the end of his letter, he wanted them to change their wrong behavior before he came so that he would not have to discipline them (2:3; 13:10).

2. A Previous Letter (2:3–11).

Paul says he had written a previous letter, one "out of great distress and anguish of heart and with many tears" (2:3–4). Is this letter 1 Corinthians? Or is it 2 Corinthians 10–13 that has been misplaced? Or is it a lost letter? At least one correspondence sent to the Corinthians is no longer available, a letter sent before 1 Corinthians (1 Cor. 5:9). If 1 Corinthians were to be this letter "of tears," then 1 Corinthians 16:5–6 would be Paul's reference to his future plans and 1 Corinthians 5 would refer to the same person as in 2 Corinthians 2:5–11. Philip E. Hughes, in his *New International Commentary on the New Testament*, ably defends 1 Corinthians as that previous letter. Others posit that such a letter written between 1 and 2 Corinthians is no longer extant. Therefore, Paul wrote at least four letters to the Corinthians, two of which were not preserved. The previous letter may be 1 Corinthians or a lost letter. However, as to its being 1 Corinthians, we find it unlikely that Paul would command the Corinthians to hand someone over to Satan (1 Cor. 5:5) and then admonish them for administering too heavy a punishment (2 Cor. 2:6–7). In addition, could 1 Corinthians really be called a letter of *"great* distress *(thlipsis)* and *anguish* of heart and with *many* tears?" If 2 Corinthians 10–13 were the letter of tears, then Paul still would not have fulfilled his promise to visit in 2 Corinthians 13:1! Even as we do not know for certain all the details of Paul's troubles in Asia, we may not know the details of this person who sinned and was over-punished.

Even if 1 Corinthians 5 is not the situation mentioned in 2 Corinthians 2, when teaching or practicing discipline in the church both passages need to be studied simultaneously. Sexual immorality is a sin that affects an entire congregation (the "body" of Christ [1 Cor. 6:18–20]). Therefore, congregations need to lovingly discipline persons who commit such sins, so that their spirit may be saved at the last day of judgment. Simultaneously, punishments can be overly severe, and people can be destroyed by "excessive sorrow" (2:7). Forgiveness and mercy and love are all qualities of God, "the Parent of compassion." Why must so many of us err on the side of complete laxity or on the side of complete severity? Love is the final foundation for action—whether to forgive or to discipline or to do both.

3. *The Open Door (2:12–17).*

Paul narrates this letter not along topics or themes. Rather, he uses a chronological schema and inserts along the way theological truths that these different events teach. In 1:3–11, Paul speaks of the troubles in Asia and what they taught about comfort and suffering. In 1:15–17 he speaks of his plans to go to Macedonia, and the importance of trust and love. In 2:12–13 he moves to Troas, a seaport town in Asia across from Macedonia, and discusses the truths he learned there. In 7:5–7 he has now crossed the Aegean Sea into Macedonia and found Titus. In 8:17 Paul begins to envision future travel south to the province of Achaia. In 10:2 he envisions his entrance into Corinth itself. Second Corinthians might thus be understood as a motion picture or a talk, illustrated by a map of the Mediterranean countries, which is periodically halted to explain what was happening in the participants' minds at each place.

Paul is still showing how his behavior toward the Corinthians is motivated by his great love for them. All his behavior is motivated by love. He had gone into Troas for the express purpose of preaching the good news of Christ. "The Lord had opened a door for me," or literally "a door for me had been opened in the Lord," indicates that Paul had found a place and an opportunity to preach (2:12). Often Paul would preach at a synagogue since ancient Jewish worship leaders would invite visitors to speak a word to the congregation after the Scripture readings (e.g., Acts 13:15). At Ephesus he taught daily in the lecture hall of Tyrannus (Acts 19:9). Paul does not mention any further specifics about the place in Troas, since it is not germane to this communication. He does add that this place and opportunity were "in the Lord," which means that they were not created for Paul's self-interest.

Often, Christians today use an "open door" as a test by which to decide whether God wants them to do a certain action. An "open door" is an opportunity. But for Paul it was often a situation that had more hardships, as in Ephesus where "a great door for effective work has opened to me, and *there are many who oppose me*" (1 Cor. 16:9). At Troas, Paul had this "open door" yet he did not avail himself of it, but sailed over to Macedonia. Paul's action teaches us today that we cannot allow "open door" opportunities to be our ultimate criteria for decisions. More important than opportunities are relationships.

Paul "had no peace of mind" because he did not find Titus at Troas. Apparently, Titus and Paul had agreed on meeting again at this city. Paul would have been traveling in Asia north from Ephesus to Troas while Titus would have been traveling in Macedonia south to Achaia and returning north again to Macedonia, sailing back to Troas. Paul describes Titus as "my brother." These appellatives were no casual terms, but they indicated Paul's great love for Titus. Paul may never have married, but through his worship of Jesus the Messiah he adopted a new family. Therefore, he now had new brothers and sisters, mothers and fathers, and children. Titus was his "brother" and a colleague in ministry. Greater in importance to Paul than any possible new converts were his "brothers" in the Lord: Titus (2:13) and the Corinthians (1:8). Paul's concern for his coworker and the new believers at Corinth was more important than potential believers and keeping to his original goal—to preach at Troas. How different Paul was to some Christians who seek only new converts and have little interest in the well-being of other believers! Titus had gone to the Corinthians to determine their spiritual state (7:7) and to prepare them for the forthcoming gathering of funds for the famine-affected Christians in Judea (8:6). When Paul saw that Titus had not returned and no one had word of him, he "said good-by," leaving others to minister at Troas, and crossed the sea into Macedonia trying to find Titus and news of the Corinthians.

If the Corinthians complained about Paul's fickleness in his plans to visit Corinth, the Asians might also have complained of his irresponsibility at Troas. Paul goes on to develop the rationale for his action at Troas in chapter 3, but since he is taking us on a journey of his spirit, he breaks forth into a triumphant benediction in 2:14–17. The benediction presages the news Paul will share in 7:6–7, God "comforted [Paul and Timothy] by the coming of Titus, and not only by his coming but also by the comfort [the Corinthians] had given him."

Paul alludes to the image of a triumphant general. After a victorious battle, the spoils, captives, general, and army would all parade into the city that had sent them out to fight. Tablets would be carried that listed the spoils and pictured the different battles. After the captives but before the victorious general in a chariot, incense bearers would walk,[2] releasing fragrant odors, somewhat as in years past ticker tape used to be thrown out of windows down on parading soldiers. The victors would also sacrifice in thanksgiving to the gods before and after the parade. God here is the general. Paul and his coworkers are the army. Even though they felt as if they had received the death sentence (1:9), they ended up living, and being the victors. This God in

---

[2] For descriptions of triumphal processions see Appian's *Roman History VIII*, "The Punic Wars" 9:66; XII "The Mithridatic Wars" 17:117; Josephus, *Jewish War* VII, 5:4–6; Plutarch's *Lives*, "Aemilius Paulus" XXXII–XXXIV.

whom all promises are "Yes" also is the General who *always* wins, no matter how despairing the way may seem. People can defect from the army, but those who remain will always be on the winning side.

Spices were carried by the incense bearers, therefore they would "spread everywhere the fragrance." But Paul develops the image further. Not only are Christians the army, they are the very fragrance itself, "we are the aroma" (2:15). The fragrance would drift back to the general and the army and sideways to the spectators. "Fragrance" (*osmē*; 2:14, 16) may refer to any odor, whether foul or fragrant. "Aroma" (*euōdia*; 2:15) is always a sweet smell or bouquet, especially of sacrifices. "To God" Paul and his coworkers were always a *sweet* aroma. Why? Because they represented "Christ." They were the sweet fragrance of incense or of living sacrifices. This aroma did two things simultaneously. To people being saved, it caused them to receive more life. To those perishing (the captives?), it caused them to get that much closer to death. The aroma worked as a catalyst furthering a process that had already begun in others.

Paul teaches us that we cannot measure the effectiveness of our work by people's responses. Responses are determined by people's own will, their own desire to repent or not to repent. That is why numbers or monetary response are always insufficient criteria for success. But we can measure our effectiveness by whether what we say and do indeed accurately represent Christ and the message revealed by God. In other words, we must ask, "Is our fragrance from Christ?" Have we spoken out God's message, as Paul says, literally, "from God before God in Christ we speak" (2:17)? Have we given life to the living, and death to the dying rather than vice versa?

Paul summarizes this first section of his letter by referring again to his and his coworkers' pure motives ("sincerity," 2:17; 1:12) and by alluding to what they are not. In 1:24 Paul had explained that he and his coworkers do not "lord it over" the Corinthians' faith, the same root word that Jesus used in Matthew 20:25. Now Paul adds in 2:17 that many "peddle" the word of God. A "peddler" was a petty retail dealer who would sell by hawking something. To "peddle the word of God" may refer to getting excessive financial gain from teaching or preaching, or it may refer to corrupting or adulterating God's teachings to sell the product more. What distinguishes genuine preachers is their purity of motive. They aim to please God by loving those whom they serve (2:4). Therefore, their message will not always be well received by all people, but it will always be well received back by the Sender (2:15–17).

For Further Study

1. Read through 2 Corinthians making two lists: What does "good" conduct in God's grace look like, and what does "worldly" conduct look like?

2. Discuss what possible changes you may have to make to balance (a) your word to do something or your reliability with (b) your love for others or your flexibility.

3. Make a list of all the attributes of God in 2 Corinthians and how they affect human action.

Chapter 3

Paul's Explanation: Our Competence Comes from God
(2 Corinthians 3:1–5:21)

Paul has raised a question in 2:16 which he has yet to answer fully: "And who is equal to such a task?" Who can represent Christ so well that only other people's desire to repent or not to repent affects the communication? Who can genuinely want people to grow and mature spiritually (rather than keep them dependent on oneself)? Who can love people so much that, if necessary, they will ignore opportunities to speak publicly in Christ's behalf? Who can love people so much that they will *not* use God's Word for their own financial and ambitious benefit? Who can speak God's message approved by God? Who can restrain from evaluating themselves *only* by people's positive responses? "And, who is sufficient for these things?" If in chapters 1 and 2 Paul defends himself and his associates as having behaved with pure motives, in chapters 3 through 5 he shows that their competence to lead comes from God.

A. God's Covenant Written on Living Hearts Causes Frankness (3:1–18)

Paul brings to the fore the dilemma in which the Corinthians have placed him. His leadership has been fundamentally questioned. If he defends himself before their sight, they will feel superior to him. And apparently the Corinthians have decided that the most impressive leaders do come with letters of recommendation.

1. Letters of recommendation (3:1–6).

Paul uses in 3:1–2 the technical phrase "letters of recommendation." He uses the verb form in Romans 16:1–2 when he introduces Phoebe to the churches in Rome. The ancients would use letters of recommendation even as we do today, but with some modifications. These letters would ask a favor for the person introduced ("I ask you to receive [Phoebe] in the Lord in a way worthy of the saints and to give her any help she may need from you") and cite reasons why the recipient should grant the favors requested ("for she has been a great help to [or leader over] many people, including me"). Paul's Letter to Philemon, Apphia, Archippus, and the church in their home might also be considered a letter of recommendation, a lengthier one recommending that they welcome back Onesimus in the same manner they would welcome Paul back (v. 17). In our contemporary society letters of recommendation tend to be mailed, and recommenders tend *not* to want to show their letters to the person recommended (or not recommended!). In contrast, in the first century letters of introduction or recommendation were customarily carried by the person concerned, probably since the first century had no publicly available postal system. Writers also would indicate the carrier, as in, "Hermophilos, who is delivering the letter to you, is . . . "[1]

"Or do we need, *like some people*, letters of recommendation to you or from you?" Paul's question certainly suggests that the Corinthians were in contact with some people who did have letters of introduction. Why should they not have been the superapostles? The Corinthians were so impressed with these letters that they were apparently suggesting that Paul and his coworkers obtain some. Paul's question demands a "no" answer. He and his team do *not* need a letter of recommendation to them or from them, because they already have one. In addition, Paul's answer explains why his refusal to preach at Troas was absolutely essential.

If Paul should astonish his readers with the possibility that Christians could themselves be "aromas" (2:15–16), here he

---

[1] Clinton W. Keyes, "The Greek Letter of Introduction," *American Journal of Philology* LVI (1935), 35.

astounds them again with the possibility that they are "letters" (3:2). The Corinthians already have letters and these letters are *themselves*! Why did Paul refuse to preach at Troas? He left Troas for Macedonia because the goal of his ministry was to enable the people with whom he served to be his "letter of recommendation." Paul had no measly papyrus. He had a living dossier!

Most ancient mail was carried by friends or relatives when they travelled. "Are you going to Rome this Elul? Do you mind bringing this letter to my dear friends Priscilla and Aquila?" Government officials had their own couriers who would run quickly from city to city. Sometimes couriers with important messages would place signs on their chests so they could run unhindered.

The couriers or messengers are Paul and Timothy. They are running with a message from their Ruler and going to their Ruler ("we speak before God . . . sent from God" 2:17). That message or letter is the Corinthians themselves. They have only *one* letter because although the Corinthians may want to divide into many factions, in God's sight they are one, a community of interdependent people, one sanctuary for the presence of God (1 Cor. 6:19; 12:1–27). The message is not simply placed on their chests, but it is cut into the hearts of these messengers ("written on our hearts" 2:12). "Engraving" is a way for Paul to express the great affection he and his associates have for the Corinthians. This letter is visible to everyone, even as Paul's letters are meant to be understood fully (1:13). Even though the Corinthians' faces are engraved on their chests, the letter is from Christ, written with the ink of the Spirit of the living God (3:3). The message belongs not to Paul. Paul and Timothy are simply the couriers.

The other image that might fit the extended metaphor in 2 Corinthians 3:1–3 comes from Exodus 32:15–19. Since Paul will be alluding to the old covenant in a few lines, here he may be suggesting that he and Timothy are messengers like Moses. As Moses carried two tablets of stone down from the Sinai mountain, so, too, Paul and Timothy carry a tablet. They carry only one tablet, the Corinthians. As with the lettering on Moses' tablets, Paul's and Timothy's tablet can be seen by everyone.

The difference is that the message Paul and Timothy carry is engraved by the Spirit on their hearts, not on stone tablets. The writing is still the writing of God, but this new message cannot be thrown and broken at the foot of any mountain.

Paul is explaining how their concern and love cannot be broken. It cannot be hidden. It is "known and read by everybody" (3:2). It cannot be destroyed. Their love is so great it distinguishes their bodies. The Corinthians are a part of Paul's very self, as he will say, "we have . . . opened wide our hearts to you" (6:11). The Corinthians themselves are proof of Christ's commission to Paul, the apostle. They are proof of Christ's work among them.

When we go about our work for Christ, we, too, need to remember that our effect on people is what counts. We, too, want our affection for those we serve to be our message. We need to help people mature in Christ so that they can become our living letters of commendation that we carry in our affection—people whom we love in a Christ-like manner, in whom God has been allowed to write that letter. Even if we begin a program that ends or sponsor an event that has few people attend, we will be successful in God's sight if we have affected people to their good and increased our own affection for them. We cannot make people mature although that might be our goal, but we can evaluate ourselves by whether we have delivered the right message. Our goal is to have living letters of recommendation. Our measure of success is whether we have spoken (and lived) true to God's word.

The means for success comes from God. Therefore, Paul and Timothy and all his other coworkers are confident. They are confident because God has made them competent. Paul describes God in 3:6 as the One who also makes his team competent ministers of a new covenant not written but spiritual. Why is a new covenant needed? "For the letter kills, but the Spirit gives life" (3:6).

2. Two Covenants (3:7–18).

When the Corinthians questioned Paul's integrity, Paul understood that they had questioned the integrity of the God Paul represented (1:17–21). Paul again sees that if the Corinthians question the nature of their effectiveness as leaders, having *living* letters of recommendation, then they have also questioned the nature of the message or covenant they proclaim, a covenant that brings life. Why would Paul raise this defense of the new covenant if he did not suspect that the Corinthians were living according to another covenant? Paul now describes the two covenants and explains why the new one gives them such hope (3:12).

In three conditional subordinate clauses Paul describes the old covenant: "the ministry of death," "the ministry of condemnation," and "[the ministry] fading away" (or "being rendered ineffective" [3:7, 9, 11]). In contrast, in three main clauses Paul describes the new covenant: "the ministry of the Spirit," "the ministry of righteousness," and "[the ministry] which lasts" (3:8, 9, 11). In the conditional clauses Paul speaks of the wonders of the old covenant. In the main clauses he speaks of the greater wonders of the new covenant. The old covenant came in a glory so great that the Israelites were not able to stare into Moses' face. The glory of the new covenant will be much greater, but its full glory remains to be manifested.

Paul immediately shows how the new covenant affects action, "we are very bold" (3:12, NIV) or "we use great plainness of speech" (KJV) or "we speak without reserve" (Weymouth). The new covenant is open and visible to all, therefore so are the new ambassadors open and visible in their actions. Why and when did Moses place a veil over his face? According to Exodus 34:29–35, Moses' face shone because he had been talking with God. God's shekinah glory was passed on to Moses. Moses placed the veil over his face *after* he had finished speaking with the people of Israel. According to Paul, he placed this veil over his face so that the people would not see the end of the glory. He did not want them to see that the radiance was temporary, "being rendered ineffective" (3:13). Moses may not have wanted the people to see that the radiance came to an end, because then they may have questioned Moses' authority. Moses may have been concerned about the fidelity and cooperation of these Israelites. They had already made a golden calf. Moses had already broken the first set of tablets. Apparently, seeing Moses' face shine created a fear in the people—a right, if basic, reaction to God. This fear may be all that Moses had to use to spur the people on to worship the one living God.

Paul and his associates do not have to veil their faces. They do not have to veil their message. They are free. Every believer in the new covenant has an unveiled face because the glory received from the Lord is continually increasing but not decreasing. Again, we all have "one face" because we are the one body of Christ (3:18). We, as it were, look into a mirror. In that mirror looks out the Lord. As we gaze into the Lord's face, we are slowly being transformed to look like the Person we behold.

B. God's Mercy Encourages Paul in Hard Times (4:1–5:10)

Now that Paul has described the ever more glorious new covenant that he and his coworkers preach, he returns again to the significance for their living. The goal of ministry is to affect the living by giving them life because they believe in a life-giving covenant (3:1–6). Moreover, Paul and his coworkers are open and frank in their work because they believe in a covenant made visible to all, which never loses its glory (3:12–18).

1. God's Mercy does not Result in Deception (4:1–6).

In 4:1 Paul continues writing about the openness of their work, but adds the additional ramification of this new covenant, "we do not lose heart" (4:1). He and his coworkers do not become discouraged or tire of their work. *Egkakeo* may mean not only "lose heart" but also "behave badly or remissly." In that case, Paul would be saying that having received this covenant of mercy that changes his team members' inner natures to be like the character of the Lord of the covenant, they do not behave badly. This latter translation corresponds well with the contrast to come, "secret and shameful ways" (4:2). In the same way, when Luke describes Jesus' parable of the persistent widow as one that teaches them about the need to pray with continued trust, "not become weary" may be better translated as "not behave badly" (Luke 18:1). In the parable, the elect might lose faith because the wrongs done to them by their unrighteous opponents have not been avenged.

What type of behavior is totally inconsistent with this new

covenant? "Secret and shameful ways" are not possible if one
believes in the covenant of "ever-increasing glory" (3:18; 4:2).
Paul explains what he means by "secret and shameful" in the
descriptive phrase that follows, "not walking in deception, nor
distorting the word of God" (4:2). "Deception" refers to
"knavery" and the "adulteration of drugs or money." "Distorting" also refers to adulterating incense or wine, beguiling,
ensnaring, taking by craft.

Paul develops the same concept he has introduced in 2:17:
"peddle the word of God for profit." In other words, Paul and
his associates have not deceived the Corinthians by adding
"alloys" to their message. They have not changed God's
revelation in such a way as to benefit themselves and unfairly
attract the Corinthians. They have preached the unadulterated
message they received from God. Deception and distortion,
Paul implies, are characteristics of the ways of those who oppose
him. Paul will tell the Corinthians more bluntly in 2 Corinthians 11:3 that distortion was a characteristic of the serpent, which
caused Eve's deception. (The Corinthians are in Eve's place just
before she ate the fruit.) Distortion is also a characteristic of the
wise whose wisdom does not come from God (1 Cor. 3:19).
Distortion also characterized the spies who had tried to trick
Jesus, giving reason for the envious teachers of the law and chief
priests to arrest Jesus (Luke 20:23). They did not really want to
know, "Is it right for us to pay taxes to Caesar or not?" Rather,
they wanted to ask Jesus a question that could not be answered
without offending someone. Jesus saw through their duplicity
and kept the spies from trapping him. Paul, too, saw the
duplicity of his opponents and was seeking to reveal the truth.

Paul had said that he and his team were "the smell of
death" to those who are perishing (2:15–16). One reason their
message is perceived by some as "death" is that the sight of
people who have rejected God's message has been blinded by
"the god of this age"—Satan. The good news is hidden only to
these people, but not because the good news is in any way a
secret knowledge. The good news is delivered in an honest and
clear fashion, but it cannot always be understood. This veil or
distorted sight keeps them from seeing the shekinah glory of
Christ.

Paul treats God as One God, not three. We Christians often treat God more as three Gods rather than as one God in three Persons. Even as the Lord Christ is the Spirit (3:17–18), so, too, Christ is "the image of God" (4:4). Although this Greek word for "image" is the same one used to describe humans made in the "image" of God (*eikōn*, Gen 1:26; 5:1 LXX), in this context Christ's glory is unique. Christ is more than a mirror image of God. Christ is the living image or representation of God. If the "image" of humans reflects God in the same way as the "image" of Christ reflects God, then indeed Paul and his associates could "preach themselves" (4:5). But since Christ is the living image of God, humans must look to Christ to get God's glory, and therefore must preach "Jesus Christ as Lord" (4:5).

Verse 4:5 is a great summary of the style of leadership Paul and his coworkers maintain, "For we do not preach ourselves, but Jesus Christ as Lord, and ourselves as your servants for Jesus' sake." This transition sentence both summarizes the previous chapters and introduces the section to come. So far Paul has explained that to "preach ourselves" is to use deception and to distort God's word (4:2; 2:17; 1:12). To "preach ourselves" is impossible if the preacher wants the listeners to receive the glory that comes from God. If indeed the preacher elevates and highlights Jesus Christ as Master, then the preacher must be the slave of others for the sake of this great Master. No matter how frequently we mouth "Servant Leader" as a concept of leadership (the leader who serves others), frequently we live by "Man [sometimes Woman] with a Mission," "A Person Set Aside," "A Special Person." Respecting and appreciating leaders gets twisted into undue attention and reverence. As was once said of a famous "devout" rock and roll singer, "He is too important a person to have to live by everyday morality [i.e., not committing adultery]." The glory that comes from Christ, which is then reflected onto the human face, can get misunderstood. The listener or the preacher can begin to think that that *reflected* glory is not reflected at all but a *self-generated* glory, or that the reflected glory is not available to all. God's glory shines in all the hearts of all the people who have turned to the Lord (3:16; 4:6).

"Slaves of others" is a metaphor; it is not literally true.

Greville MacDonald comments in his biography of George MacDonald that churches are in "danger of treating their minister as if he were their servant instead of Christ's."[2] No Christian should enslave another. However, because of the marvelous light that we receive, we are freed and we are strengthened to serve others voluntarily "for Jesus' sake." Paul does here say that they are the servants of the Corinthians. But his Lord is Jesus, not the Corinthians. Jesus is the Lord who sends his slaves to take care of a neighbor's problems. The slaves may be helping the neighbor, but they are under directives from their own Master. The source of the glory must always be appreciated. It is the "glory of God in the face of Christ" (4:6).

2. *Treasure in Jars of Clay (4:7–18).*

Paul concludes the transition paragraph 4:1–6 with a sentence in which a synonym for "light" recurs four times, "For God, who said, 'Let *light shine* out of darkness,' made his *light shine* [one word in Greek] in our hearts to give us the *light*" (4:6). Where is this magnificent light stored? In a clay pot! Here is another paradox for the Christian life. A clay pot cannot reveal what is inside. A great treasure (God's glory) is stored in a fragile container. Corinth used to have a potters' quarter one mile west of its center. No doubt the Corinthians would use these clay pots frequently. Often precious treasures would be hidden in cheap and fragile containers. Although in Roman triumphal processions (2:14) gold and silver would often be exhibited "for show," the treasure of God's glory is hidden in clay containers. Clay containers are used "to show that this all-surpassing power is from God and not from us" (4:7). Their competency *must* come from God. No one can confuse the treasure and its container if the container is no treasure itself. The "extraordinary quality of the power" of Paul and his coworkers must come from God, and not be self-generated.

What are the clay containers? They are defined in 4:8–9. Paul does not here write about physical bodies. The clay containers are more specifically the life of difficulties arising

[2]*George MacDonald and His Wife* (London: George Allen & Unwin, 1924), p. 178.

from external and internal opposition to genuine Christian ministry: "We are hard pressed on every side, but not crushed; perplexed, but not in despair; persecuted, but not abandoned; struck down, but not destroyed" (4:8–9). Paul has several such lists of trials in the Corinthian correspondence: 1 Corinthians 4:9–13; 2 Corinthians 4:7–10; 6:1–10; 11:18–12:10. In each of these lists Paul describes a slightly different aspect of the same topic, the lifestyle of a true Christian leader, with the same answer, a list of difficulties.

In 1 Corinthians 4, Paul explains how he and Apollos function as "servants of Christ" (4:1) since they are both Christian leaders. Consequently, the Corinthians have no reason to create dissensions by choosing between them. The apostles who are "first" (1 Cor. 12:28), and who should be imitated (4:16), are not like the "arrogant people" who talk (4:19). Rather, their "power" (4:19) is revealed in following Christ's own sufferings. First Corinthians 4:9–13 focuses on the present low esteem in which the apostles are held. Second Corinthians 4:7–10 focuses on why such low esteem is really necessary—to show that God is the source of power.

These lists of difficulties are written in a magnificent style reflecting the magnificence of the treasure they describe. The grammarian A. T. Robertson considers that 1 Corinthians 4, and 2 Corinthians 4, 10, 11, and 13, among other chapters have "oratory of the highest kind with the soul all ablaze with great ideas. The words respond to this high environment and are all aglow with beauty and light."[3] Paul is not against rhetoric *per se*. He is against deception. Therefore, he uses his own training inspired by God. Although he may not always be spontaneous, he will always be genuine because genuineness flows from a loving and truthful spirit.

Paul first lists his difficulties in a rhythmic, forceful, and vivid parallelism. In parallelism, like is paired with like:

| in all experiencing trouble, | but not being crushed, |
| being uncertain, | but not being in great doubt, |

---

[3]Robertson, A. T., *A Grammar of the Greek New Testament in the Light of Historical Research* (Nashville: Broadman, 1934), p. 1198.

being persecuted,	but not being abandoned,
being thrown down,	but not being killed
	(2 Cor. 4:8).

In Paul's Greek text the first and last phrase each have one word separated by the conjunctions "but not." Trouble, uncertainty, persecution, and being thrown down are synonyms that all contrast with not being crushed, doubting, being abandoned, and being killed. Paul repeats "but not" four times, heightening the paradoxes of the Christian life, making his list all the more rhythmic, passionate, and vivid. The discursive explanation of verse 7 has broken out into this surprising, powerful listing of exactly what is entailed in "clay containers": trouble, uncertainty, persecution, attack. If the Corinthians, like us, may have been attracted to the positive imagery of light in 4:6, they too, like us, may have been shocked by Paul's contrasting negative list in 4:8–10. Paul writes with emotion and vividness because he reacts with emotion and vividness to the events he has had to experience. He does not embrace these difficulties for their own sake.

The parallel phrases and the repetitious sounds of participles mirror the closeness of the concepts of trouble, uncertainty, persecution, and being thrown down. The adversative "but not" distinguishes these concepts. The manifestation of God's power (4:7) comes when trouble (which is so close to destruction) does not degenerate into destruction, uncertainty does not degenerate into despair, persecution does not leave one abandoned, and being hurled down does not produce death. The images to which Paul alludes are quite physical: pressure, crushing, throwing. The extraordinary quality of God's power prevents the natural human result.

Paul builds up to a climax that is in verse 10. Instead of short rhythmic synonymous parallel phrases, Paul uses two lengthy parallel clauses: "We always carry around in our body the death of Jesus, so that the life of Jesus may also be revealed in our body." What personal advantage can Paul and his coworkers have if they carry their treasure in jars of clay full of difficulties? What exactly have they been carrying about? Why must they experience trouble? They carry about the *death* of

Jesus. Here is Paul's final paradox in this list: Because they carry the "death" of Jesus in their bodies, now "the life of Jesus" can be revealed. The perfect parallelism is broken by the addition of the pronoun "our." "Our" body will not have revealed in it Jesus' life, if Jesus' death has not been previously carried. The imagery of "life" hearkens back to the "light" and "glory" of 4:6 and the "treasure" in 4:7.

Paul leaves the reader with a vivid image in 4:10. "Death" is personified as a dead person whom people must carry. Who wants to carry a cold, stiff, heavy corpse? Paul uses "carry around," not simply "carry," to accentuate that such a burden occurs "always" or "at all times." Indeed, Paul alludes to the very image Jesus used: to bear a cross, except that here that cross is no longer wood but a Wood-Carver, the carpenter himself. That "cross" is experiencing trouble, being uncertain, being persecuted, being thrown down. But even as God spoke and out of darkness commanded light, so the dead body we carry becomes a living body within our own body. The dead carpenter is revealed to be the living Lord. And if the dead carpenter becomes the living Lord, so, too, like the carpenter, those who carry the carpenter will themselves be resurrected and receive life (4:14).

Paul explains that this type of ministry is for the benefit of the Corinthians. Paul's life of difficulties helps him to reach more and more people (4:15). The Corinthians' prayers will increase thanksgiving to God (1:11). Their increasing life will also increase thanksgiving to God (4:15).

Paul summarizes chapter 4 by repeating the same verb in 4:16 he used in 4:1: "Therefore, we do not lose heart." The "outward" physical nature (4:16) that after the late twenties in most people begins to deteriorate (muscle tone, responses, memory, all-around health), is a symbol for the difficulties from external and internal opposition to genuine Christian ministry that Paul has cited in 4:8–9. Even as the body begins to deteriorate so that a person may look less "glorious" (some of our readers may be the exception and look more glorious!), in the same way Christians who have to undergo difficult circumstances may also not look very impressive. Genuine Christians need not be discouraged because their "inside" nature, their truthful nature that reflects Christ's life and glory, is being renewed day by day (4:2, 10; 3:18). Therefore the troubles, uncertainty, persecution, being thrown down of 4:8–9 become "momentary, insignificant" troubles in light of the inward change that looks forward to "an extraordinary degree—to excess—fullness of glory" (4:17). Paul writes here of a great deal of glory! Paul and his associates look forward to this unseen but eternal reward—to be in the likeness of Jesus—in order to keep in perspective the seen and outward yet impressive (in a temporary way) glory of this age, the deceptive distortion that gets immediate results. (No wonder we cannot judge effectiveness by temporary results!)

3. Earthly Tent (5:1–10).

Paul's contrast between the outward and the inward person, what is seen and what is not seen, continues in a discussion of the earthly versus the heavenly tent. Paul could be speaking of the contrast between the individual physical body and the spiritual body at death, or the contrast between the corporate "body" of Christians while on earth and the corporate body in the new earth. Some commentators have suggested that "being naked" (5:2–4) refers to an interim state between death and the resurrection. Paul fears to be a spirit apart from the body.

Since Paul had been discussing the nature of his ministry in chapter 4 and will clearly turn to this topic in 5:11, probably this paragraph should refer to the same topic. "Earthly tent" literally is "the earthly house of tent" that Paul contrasts to "the building of God" (5:1). "House" in the New Testament can refer to a literal house, a dwelling place such as the house on the rock or the house on the sand (Matt. 7:24, 26). It can also refer to a household, the inmates of the house, an extended family with laborers such as the "house" of Stephana (1 Cor. 16:15) or the "house" of Caesar (Phil. 4:22).

Paul qualifies the kind of house about which he writes by calling it "of tent." This noun for "tent" or "hut" occurs only here in the New Testament (*skēnos*). It can also refer to the body as the tabernacle of the soul or to a dead body or corpse. For Philo the tent or tabernacle (more precisely the holy place) is itself the soul because it is unseen. "Nakedness" arises in a mind "clothed neither in vice nor in virtue" (The Worse Attacks the Better XVII; Allegorical Interpretation II, XV; On Drunkenness XXXIII; On the Change of Names V). Many ancient Greeks believed that the soul was good whereas the body or matter was evil. For example, in Poseidonian Stoicism, when people were ruled by passions, their souls would become encrusted with a mudlike substance. Therefore, at death, their souls would rise up only as far as the heavy air surrounding the earth. If people controlled their passions, their souls would rise up to the moon. The better that one lived, the better one's situation would be at death. Great moral philosophers such as Plato or Socrates would have their souls rise up as high as the fixed stars where they would hear the music of the spheres, the sound of everything working beautifully "in its order."

Even today many people believe in a soul as a separate substance within the body. Experiments have been done to prove the existence of the soul by showing that people weigh less after death. However, the "soul" is used in the Bible *not* as a substance within the body but to refer to a total living person. A soul is "you." For example, Paul says that Epaphroditus "almost died for the work of Christ, risking his *life* to make up for the help [the Philippians] could not give [Paul]" (Phil 2:30), and "There will be tribulation and distress for every human *being* who does evil" (Rom. 2:9). In 1 Corinthians 15:45, Paul contrasts the first Adam, "a living being" (*soul*) with the last Adam, "a life-giving *spirit*." Does Paul in 2 Corinthians 5 show that he has accepted or adopted the Greek idea that the body is evil? He says, "while we are in this tent, we groan and are burdened" (5:4). At a minimum he cannot have fully accepted the idea that the body is evil because, he says, we will be "clothed" with a "heavenly dwelling" whereas if matter is evil, no dwelling would be necessary at all. What Paul says in 2 Corinthians 5:2 would agree with his words in 1 Corinthians 15:44, a "natural body" will be sown, a "spiritual *body*" will be reaped.

In 2 Corinthians 5:4 Paul definitely contrasts mortality with life. "Pitching a tent" is used metaphorically by John to describe the incarnation of Jesus. The Word "made his dwelling" is literally, "the Word pitched its tent" (John 1:14). "Tent," *skēnē*, is never specifically used of an individual body in the New Testament, although skēnē is adapted to *skēnōma* to denote a living body in 2 Peter 1:13–14. "Eternal tents" can refer to heaven (Luke 16:9), as does the "true tent" or "tabernacle," God's dwelling place (Heb. 8:2; Rev. 21:3).

Paul may be using the idea of an "earthly tent" to refer to a physical, mortal body in contrast to a spiritual body, the one received at the resurrection. Or, he could be using "earthly tent" to refer more generally to life, in contrast to heaven or the new earth. Considering that Paul as a tentmaker may very well have lived sometimes in his own tent as opposed to a permanent building, the contrast between "earthly tent" and "building" is quite striking. The tent is made by human hands and it is slowly falling apart. God's dwelling is not made by humans, and therefore it is eternal.

Paul says that we desire "to put on over" ourselves our heavenly dwelling (5:2, 4). It is as if the heavenly dwelling were a cloak to wear. Paul here speaks either of a resurrected body or of eternal life that would remove him and his associates from all the great difficulties they experience in their ministry. Being "naked," then, is Paul's present mortal state—literally, being susceptible to cold and illnesses, metaphorically, being susceptible to unfair accusations. If Paul had the glory of eternal life or a resurrected body, he would not have to endure what he now endures. He is indeed burdened by anxiety for the preservation of his work. (See also Rom. 8:20–24.) The desire for eternal life that Paul and we have is a good one because God has made us for this purpose and has given the presence of the Holy Spirit "as a deposit, guaranteeing" (5:5) that indeed our mortal state is temporary. Yet that desire cannot be fulfilled until we are in Christ's presence.

"As long as we are at home in the body we are away from the Lord" (5:6) would not then refer to having or not having a physical body. We will always have a body. Rather "to be at home in the body" means to feel complete satisfaction and comfort in this life. If someone feels completely content in this life, then that person is not looking forward to being in Christ's presence, as expressed in the hymn "Pilgrimage Canticle":

Water
    running
       from the mountain
lemming—
    downward
      to the sea
And the
    old men
      see a symbol
what they
    wish
      it to be:
"Welcome brother to your homeland,"
thus they comforted me.
But the
    home that
      I will cherish
    is but
      a memory.
Different water rushes by me,
different grass lives beneath my feet.
In this
    world of
      friendly strangers
but a
    pilgrim
      I will be.
Lord, walk with me.

However, whether one is in a mortal state or an eternal one, one can always aspire to be pleasing in the Lord's sight. To please God is Paul's ultimate goal and it should be the goal for every genuine Christian. No matter what our present state, situation, or place, we can always aim to please God. If we are becoming more and more like Jesus (3:18), we would want to please Jesus. Moreover, "all" of us "must" appear before the "judgment seat of Christ" (5:10). The judgment seat (*bēma*) was a raised platform in the agora of many cities. It still stands at Corinth. The proconsul Lucius Julius Gallio probably sat on this platform when he heard the complaints about Paul (Acts 18:12). Judicial decisions would be made from this seat. Judges would also carry with them ivory seats from which to make their judgments. Paul pictures Jesus as on such a seat, "God's judgment seat" (Rom. 14:10). Paul says here that all persons at death will be judged by how they lived their lives. No one can avoid this judgment. As the writer of Hebrews says, we are "destined to die once, and after that to face judgment" (Heb. 9:27). So if a desire "to please" the Lord (5:9) is not a sufficient motivation to work for God's unseen kingdom, then perhaps "fear" of the Lord at judgment should suffice (5:11).

C. Corinthians Should Be Proud of Paul and His Team (5:11–21)

Paul returns again to mention directly his main goal in this letter—to defend his and his team's leadership. Paul and his associates do fear the Lord. Therefore they want to persuade people, but again, always in God's sight, or with a desire to please God ultimately (5:11). Paul's main goal in this letter might be picked up from 5:11: "I hope [what we are] is plain to your conscience." Paul hopes the Corinthians might understand what he and his associates are all about, but from what he has heard from the associates who have given him news about the Corinthians, he does not think that they do understand his team's ministry goals and ways at all. Now that Paul has explained how their motives are pure and their competence comes from God to be ministers of a living covenant in the midst of difficult circumstances, the Corinthians should be proud of Paul and his coworkers.

Again, boasting is not inherently wrong. To boast or be proud of other Christians is a positive trait. Even as Jesus said whoever confesses him before others, he will confess before his Father, so too, when the Corinthians professed publicly their pride in Paul and his associates, they were confessing publicly their belief in all for which Paul stood.

1. "What is in the heart" (5:11–15).

The Corinthians should take pride in "what is in the heart," not "what is seen" (literally, "the face," 2 Cor. 5:12). "What is in the heart" would be a synonym for the "inward" (4:16), the "unseen," and the "eternal" (4:18). Paul and his associates do not need an inanimate "temporary" letter of recommendation because their letters are the Corinthians' faces engraved on their hearts. They do not preach the covenant that is fading away but rather the one that will be ever-increasing in glory. This spiritual covenant changes the heart or essence of each person. Paul and his associates may not be very impressive as they are "hard pressed," "perplexed," "persecuted," and "struck down" (4:8–9), but the Corinthians need to appreciate that this discomfort is endured because of their great love.

Before we glibly dismiss the Corinthians, we need to ask ourselves, "How often have we spoken up on behalf of someone who was not impressive but who did humbly serve God?" Or, if we did speak up, did we resent the cost to our own public esteem because we spoke up for an unpopular person or cause?

Verse 5:14 is a beautiful verse summarizing love as the motivating force behind the action of Paul and his coworkers: "For Christ's love compels us, because we are convinced that one died for all, and therefore all died." Love is an action noun. Paul can either mean that their own love *for* Christ "compels," "rules," or "controls" their behavior *or* that the love produced *by* Christ "compels," "rules," or "controls" them. "Compel" literally means "encircle," "embrace," "to hold or keep together, confine, secure." Paul's and his coworkers' love *for* Christ or the love produced by Christ in them constrains or confines them so greatly that they are forced to act as they do. Conversely, their love for Christ or the love produced by Christ encircles them, embraces them, holds or keeps them secure. "Their own love *for* Christ" probably is what Paul intends because he adds "because we are convinced." Because Paul and the others had come to the conclusion that "one died for all, and therefore all died" (5:14), they are filled with a great love for Christ that motivates all their action, their resulting love for the Corinthians. But even if Paul here writes of their love *for* Christ, this love is a result of *Christ's* loving action—one dying for all, which released all to live for Christ.

Paul writes that "One" (Christ) in behalf of "all" died, not that One in behalf of "some" died. John has a similar thought in his first letter: "[Jesus Christ] is the atoning sacrifice for our sins, and not only for ours but also for the sins of the whole world" (2:2). Christ died for everyone, not only for the elect, the persons who would become believers. Christ's magnanimous love expressed in the crucifixion-death is all the more magnanimous because it is offered to all, both to those "who take pride in what is seen" and also to those who will take pride in "what is in the heart." Christ is a synecdoche, a part who represents all. When Christ died, every human being died. No humans need to die to cleanse them from the evil they have done. They have died already, represented in Christ's death. Why did Christ die in behalf of all? Christ died in order that "the living no longer to themselves may live but [they may live] to the One having died and having risen in behalf of them" (5:15). The One died for all so that all may live for One. Paul had already explained that he and his associates do not abandon their faith in Jesus when they have difficult circumstances, because they then learn to rely on the life-giving power of Jesus (1:9; 4:11). Here he adds that they devote their life to pleasing God out of love. Since they have, in effect, "died," they cannot live to please themselves, because then they would be striving to please a dead person. Some of the Corinthians may indeed have been living "to themselves." Paul will directly confront them in 6:1: "we urge you not to receive God's grace in vain."

2. The Ministry of Reconciliation (5:16–21).

Christ "died for *all*," therefore causing genuine Christians to treat no one "from a worldly point of view" or, literally, "according to [the] flesh" (5:16). What might it mean to know someone according to the flesh? To know Christ "according to the flesh" might include seeing Christ "through a veil," missing the glory that is captured in Christ's lowly life (chs. 3 and 4). Possibly, then, knowing anyone "according to the flesh" in this context means to miss the reflecting glory that is hidden behind a life of difficulties and a life of mortality. People in Christ might be "a new creation," but they still may not look impressive.

Paul is placing a wedge between a person's previous life outside of Christ and current life "in Christ." The difference between the two is as great as the difference between an old and a new creation: "the old has gone, the new has come!" (5:17). All of this new creation comes from God whom Paul describes as "the One having reconciled us to himself through Christ" (5:18). "Reconcile" literally referred to changing money and to exchanging one thing for another. In ancient Greece "to reconcile" could refer to exchanging prisoners. Metaphorically, "reconcile" referred to changing a person from enmity to friendship. Humans are enemies of God because they continue to violate God's commands (5:19). However, God has taken the initiative to change the nature of our relationship, changing it from one of enmity to one of friendship. As the early Hebrews learned, the result of disobeying God's laws is death (e.g., Num. 16). God's reconciliation was "through Christ" who took the place of all humans, receiving their intended death. Paul does not stop here. In this passage several times he goes back and forth between describing God and then describing God's people, the new creation.

What God did becomes the model for this new creation. Now that God reconciled, God "gave us the ministry of reconciliation" (5:18). If "reconciliation" referred to exchanging money, then God did not "credit to our account" all our transgressions or sins (5:19). If God had charged us for all our action that is displeasing to God's perfect goodness, love, and truth, then we would owe God so much that we would no longer own anything, even our own lives. Instead, God ignored all our sins because Christ took our place. God, as it were, paid all our debts, leaving us free from bankruptcy. We have a new start. Instead, we were given the task to do the same for other people—bring them from enmity with God and with one another to friendship with God and with one another. Paul's words are very similar to Jesus' parable of the unmerciful servant: "I cancelled all that debt of yours because you begged me to. Shouldn't you have had mercy on your fellow servant just as I had on you?" (Matt. 18:21–35).

Because of God's previous exemplary action, Paul and his associates summarize who they are and what they do: "We are therefore Christ's ambassadors, as though God were making his appeal through us" (5:20). In Greek the sentence begins "therefore in behalf of Christ we are ambassadors." Paul emphasizes *who* sends them out as ambassadors and whom they ultimately must please—Christ. They are ambassadors for someone for whom they are full of love because that person freed them from death. "We are ambassadors" properly refers in Greek (*presbeuō*) to age, "to be the elder or eldest." Since the elders of a community often were the persons who ruled that community, *presbeuō* also meant "to serve as an ambassador," at Rome, "to act as ligatus, negotiate."

In ancient Israel elders were treated with great respect. Philo, the philosopher from Alexandria who lived during Jesus' lifetime, could assume: "the sight of seniors (*presbuteros*) or instructors or rulers or parents stirs the beholders to respect for them and decent behaviour and the desire to live a life of self-control" (Embassy to Gaius I:5). When Philo and other elders were asked to go visit Gaius to stop the imperial command to place Gaius's statues in Jewish synagogues, they were acting as "ambassadors." The *presbyters* or elders of today's Presbyterian churches function as rulers of local congregations similar to those in ancient Israel. Paul also calls himself an "ambassador," but one "in chains" in Ephesians 6:20. Paul and his associates are "ambassadors" because of what Christ did for them.

How does being "ambassadors" affect their work "as though God were making his appeal through us" (5:20)? Paul and his coworkers represent God "making his *appeal*." "Appeal" (*parakaleō*) is the verb form of the noun *paraklēsis*. Both forms were used earlier in 2 Corinthians 2:8 and 1:3–7. *Parakaleō* means "to call to one's side" or, more specifically, "to summon one's friends to act as witnesses in a trial." A defense attorney, someone who pleads another's cause before a judge, would be a *paraklētos*. Paul and his associates, speaking on God's behalf, were summoning the Corinthians to become loyal witnesses. God would be as the judge or the defendant who is summoning to court the accused or the friends who should be loyal witnesses. Paul and his associates advocate on God's behalf. Their goal is friendship between Judge or Friend and accused. The basis for this ministry of reconciliation is always love (5:14; also Philemon 7). All Christians share in a ministry of reconciliation, but some, with the gift of "appeal" or "encouragement," focus on it (Rom. 12:8).

Paul then goes on to make his appeal directly: "We implore you on Christ's behalf: Be reconciled to God" (5:20). "Become friends instead of enemies with God." This command is the second direct command to the Corinthians in this letter. Paul's first command was in 2:8: "I urge you, therefore, to reaffirm your love for [the person punished]." Paul sees the Corinthians' behavior as enmity with God because they have not welcomed God's messengers, whose lives reflect their message. "Be reconciled to God" by listening to my ambassadors. The Corinthians should take pride in Paul and his associates because they speak for "what is in the heart," they speak out of love in behalf of Christ's love: "God made him who had no sin to be sin for us, so that in him we might become the righteousness of God" (5:21). "The one not having known sin—in behalf of us— sin became." Paul repeats his earlier message (5:14–15, 19). Here he accentuates what we humans can never understand fully: the ramifications, that sinless God in the incarnate Jesus took upon himself the sins of all humans past and future.

Paul alludes to the many sin offerings for atonement practiced in his own time in the Temple at Jerusalem and rehearsed for thousands of years after God's instructions to Moses. Always the priests would lay their hands on the head of the animal, the animal would be killed "at the door of the tent of meeting," the blood sprinkled as a sign of protection, but the flesh would be burned outside the camp (e.g., Exod. 29:10–14). The Day of Atonement included the additional practice of the high priest's confessing all the wrongdoing of the people while he laid both his hands on a live goat. Then the goat would "carry on itself all their sins" out into the wilderness (Lev. 16:20–22).

In this section of his letter Paul draws at least two ramifications of Christ's death: (1) people should live no longer for themselves, but for Christ "who died for them and was raised again" (5:15); (2) people should "become the righteousness of God" (5:21). Both purpose clauses begin with the same Greek preposition, "in order that." If Christ's death results paradoxically in a new way of living (5:15), now Christ's becoming "sin" results in "righteousness." Christ's death affects the way people treat one another and also what people themselves become. "Righteousness" is the characteristic of a judge. It includes both holiness and justice.

No one can "become a Christian" and not have all his behavior altered. If we believe, we will act. If we do not believe, then what we do *is* what we really believe. Paul has concluded the second section of his letter explaining how his and his coworkers' competence comes from God, with a direct exhortation for the Corinthians to change their behavior. He will develop this theme in the fourth section wherein he urges the Corinthians not to accept the grace of God in vain (6:1–9:15). In chapters 3–5 Paul has explained that competence comes from God because in this new living covenant, believers are being transformed, becoming like the One they behold. Paul's and his team's difficulties in the world prove that God must be the source of their power. And, finally, when Jesus Christ died, he released people to live for God.

For Further Study

1. If you have a good library near you, you can find a lengthy listing of ancient letters of introduction in Clinton W. Keyes, "The Greek Letter of Introduction," *American Journal of Philology* LVI (1935), 28–44. See also ch. 5, "Letters in the Ancient World," in David E. Aune, *The New Testament in Its Literary Environment* (Philadelphia: Westminster, 1987).

2. Pray that God will make you competent to serve him. What steps can you take, such as further study or experience, to cooperate with God's response to your prayer?

3. Write out the goals for your own work, separating goals (to have living letters of recommendation) from measures (to speak and live true to God's word).

4. Read through 2 Corinthians, listing all the specific commands made to the Corinthians.

5. What can you learn about reconciliation from 2 Corinthians 5:11–21 and Romans 5:1–21? What is the main point of each passage?

Chapter 4

Paul's Warning: Do Not Accept God's Grace in Vain

(2 Corinthians 6:1–9:15)

Paul begins his charges to the Corinthians in chapter 6 with a call to action. Over and over again, as we have seen, he has set out the proofs for his claim that his ministry is a pure one and therefore worthy of the Corinthians' loyalty. He opened the letter with the claim that Christ's sufferings flowed over into his own and his coworkers' lives (1:5), then followed by detailing that these sufferings occurred in Asia and took him to the verge of death (1:8ff.). But his conduct, he declares, was exemplary and was clearly explained to the Corinthians in his previous writings (1:12–14). He and his colleagues were not like "so many" trying to make a financial profit out of their ministry (2:17), and they did not come around with references and a dossier like prospective employees (3:1ff.). They did not use deception or distort God's word but were open both in people's and in God's sight (4:2–3). Hard-pressed as they suffer for Jesus but not letting the persecution destroy their ministry because they know it is benefiting the Corinthians, they remain steady beneath the blows (4:7–12).

While Paul is constructing this argument, hoping to establish beyond a doubt the validity of his claim that his ministry is pure of profit motive and authentically under the calling of Christ, he is running another contrasting thread through these pages, challenging the impure motives of his competitors and calling for repentance. In 1:11 he speaks of God's graciousness in answering prayer and giving humans aid. In 2:5 he urges, "If anyone has caused grief, he has not so much grieved me as he has grieved all of you," calling for forgiveness, a gracious human act to match God's. At the same time, he reveals that there are those who need to be corrected by the "majority" in the Corinthian congregation (2:6). In 2:9 he explains that he is testing the Corinthian obedience. In 2:17 he compares his ministry with that of frauds who are out for profit. In 3:1 he contrasts his team with "some people" who bring references, setting his ministry of the new covenant against that of the old covenant (3:7ff.). He separates his ministry from Moses' and the veil of dulled understanding that covered the minds of those in the old ministry. In 4:4 he establishes that unbelievers are those whose minds stay veiled in the old covenant way. But, he declares, Christ's glory shines through Paul's own and his coworkers' suffering like a treasure glittering inside a pot of clay (4:7ff.). A judgment, he declares, will come eventually for all (5:10) when each person's actions will be judged as good or bad by Christ.

At this point Paul, like a skillful verbal tentmaker, weaves together the two threads of thought (defensive and offensive) with which he has been working, and reveals the design of his argument. This, he contends, has all been plain to God and I am hoping it is plain to you Corinthians, too (5:11). We have not been trying to impress you by telling you of all the sufferings we have been enduring on your behalf. We have been equipping you with an answer to those who challenge us among you and to you yourselves (5:12). What Paul has done is set up two contrasting poles—his authentic ministering team against competitors out for gain whose veiled minds do not perceive the real truth. Paul has brought the Corinthians to a choice, imaging the selection Christ will make at the judgment seat in 5:10. Now Paul has the Corinthians sitting in judgment, and they must choose between Paul and his accusers, judging as Christ does whether "the things done while in the body" are good or bad. Have Paul's and his coworkers' bodies benefited from this ministry? Have they profited financially? Just look. They have been beaten and buffeted and starved and hounded nearly to death. What profit have they gained from their ministry? Paul has been providing this "display of proofs" not to get hired by the Corinthians, but so that "you can answer those who take pride in what is seen" (the visibly impressive) "rather than in what is in the heart" (the spiritually impressive that God sees) (5:12). Paul's ministry is modeled after Christ's (5:14) not after Moses', "the old has gone, the new has come" in him (5:17).

Therefore, reconciliation of the Corinthians with Paul is in actuality, he claims, reconciliation with Christ, for just as Titus was Paul's ambassador, Paul is Christ's (5:20). The running argument concludes in 5:20 with Paul urging the Corinthians to be reconciled with God through the action of Christ. And now in 6:1 he implores the Corinthians to let that gracious act of Christ's providing a way to be reconciled not be offered to them in vain because of their own non-acting. Paul himself, we have heard over and over again, availed himself of Christ's gracious action on his own behalf (e.g., 1:11; 3:6; 5:17), and he implores the Corinthians to do the same. So chapter 6 opens with a rousing charge to action, "I tell you, now is the time of God's favor, now is the day of salvation."

A. Paul's Plea: Make Room For Us in Your Hearts (6:1–7:3)

What Paul is about to ask is that the Corinthians "open wide their hearts" (6:13) to him and his coworkers—literally, "enlarge" their hearts to make room for Paul and his team and envelop them in the Corinthians' love and tangible, practical, affectionate actions. But Paul does not go right into his request, despite the fact that he has alerted them by his electrifying charge that a plea will be forthcoming. Instead, he provides two reasons for the Corinthians to seriously consider granting the request he is about to make. Be prepared to act, he is saying, and now consider this. The first reason Paul gives that the Corinthians should respond positively to his request is that Paul and his associates have wronged no one among them and therefore have not discredited the validity of their ministry. As proof Paul follows with a list, a catalog of sufferings.

1. Reason 1: Paul's list of sufferings (6:3–13).

Stylistically, the structure of Paul's persuasive list is very interesting. In a sense we could term it a structure of persuasion. Paul knows the Corinthians feel ambiguously toward him. They experience the classic approach/avoidance syndrome because enemies of Paul and Paul's gospel are among them, poisoning their minds against Paul. Yet, in the quiet moments of their hearts they remember Paul's loving, self-sacrificing acts among them. So Paul begins with a denial, "We put no stumbling block in anyone's path," assuming his adversaries' challenge and immediately beginning with its refutation. Rather than having made anyone stumble, he says, look what we have done. As the Corinthians look at what he has done, Paul uses a stylistic technique that makes the Corinthians work. The technique is called ellipsis, and it leaves out certain words, making the readers supply those words, therefore assuring that the readers will have to study the passage seriously to understand it. The omission here occurs in 6:4, and deleted are the words "we are"; for example, "we are" in great endurance; "we are" in troubles, "we are" in hardships. This assumption of the verb "to be" is a regular practice in Greek and it assures that readers must be alert and working along with the writer.

What happens as the readers supply the subject "we" and the verb "are," is that Paul sets up a repetitive series of prepositional phrases, repeating the preposition "in" eighteen times between verses 4–7a. This technique is called anaphora, and by the repetition of a pattern of words a rhythm is established. As one reads, it sets up an expectancy of each next addition to the pattern. In the same way that we listen to a drumbeat and our minds begin to pace along with the rhythm, so do the Corinthians get caught up in the pulsing presentation of Paul's list of what he has suffered for them. Then each phrase becomes increasingly stressed. As the metrical repetition satisfies the expectancy set before each line for a next downbeat to repeat the pattern, sometimes partial satisfactions like the compound objects "hardships and distresses" are thrown in for partial satisfiers. These increase the yearning of the reader for a full return. Thus, a strong emotional effect is produced.

As Paul moves through the list of sufferings, each more specific and more calamitous than the last—from the vague "endurance" and "troubles" to the concrete "beatings," "imprisonments," "riots," and, apparently the worst of horrors for the flabby, sensuous, and hedonistic Corinthians, "hard work," "sleepless nights," and "hunger" (in other words, loss of physical comfort), he moves the reader suddenly into positive virtues. "Purity" is the first, a key word that will comprise the foundational concept of his second reason. "Understanding" and "patience" follow, with Paul passing through past personal qualities to the pinnacle of his list, "the Holy Spirit." Then follow the two primal characteristics of God according to Exodus 34:6: *hesed*, that is, the sincere, everlasting love of God—God's grace; and *emeth*, that is, rock-hard truthful speech—God's faithful truth, and on to the final entry, the "power of God."

Again Paul echoes his list in 1 Corinthians 4:9–20. He will know not the word but the power of his opponents (1 Cor. 4:19). The power of Paul is displayed in the life of suffering he lives just as the power of God was displayed in the sacrificial life of Christ, the great Suffering Servant, whose final act of supreme suffering sacrifice provided the essential way of reconciliation with God. As we are patterned after Christ with a suffering into which Christ's own suffering flows, Paul is arguing, you be reconciled with us. This provides reason number one.

Paul now breaks the pattern of anaphora, reinforcing the message he has just delivered with a new series of varied phrases that begins by alternating the connecting words *dia*, "through," and *kai*, "and," and continues by alternating *hōs*, "as," with *kai*. Still employed is another constant technique called asyndeton, the deliberate omission of conjunctions between a series of related words, phrases, or clauses separated by commas. Asyndeton creates an effect of surprise. One does not expect not to have conjunctions, those familiar "buts" and "ands" connecting the last phrase in a series. The staccato-like results, a rattling of nouns by the reader as if a burst of machine gun fire had riddled the pages, creates a vivid and impassioned effect, a hurried rhythm that gives force and emotion and a poignant passion to the passage. The technique therefore impresses the details of what is said on the mind, even making the phrases seem more numerous than they are by their rhythmic and repetitive pattern. As in falling down the front door steps, the reader may have only hit five boards but he feels them all in rapid succession. So the anaphora in Paul's passage creates a marked rhythm and the asyndeta a hurried one. The

Corinthians have gotten into the ring with a master stylist, and he has laid his punches of persuasion into them with a one-two, one-two staccato burst, smashing their resistance to him and breaking up their counterarguments.

Verse 8a is set up like the Greek letter X, called *Chi*. This is called a Chiastic structure. Paul begins describing the weapons of attack (right) and defense (left) with glory, moves to dishonor, ends his one pattern, begins again with bad report, and moves outward to end with good report again. The effect of this structure is to make a listener or reader focus on the paradox of ministry. Unlike our normal mode of argumentation (parallelism), chiastic arguments carry a hearer to the extremities, the beginning and the end, and then back again to the center. The whole enormous sentence in Greek begins in 6:1 and does not end until some 143 words later in verse 10 (a difficulty so great for English readers that editors in the NIV have added five periods to help us moderns find our way through).

Throughout this sentence Paul has been taking successive pairs of two opposite concepts and making the startling statement that in God's servants such antonyms can stand together: glory and dishonor; praise and blame; genuine yet regarded as imposters; known yet unknown; dying yet living; beaten yet not killed; sorrowful yet rejoicing; poor yet rich; having nothing yet possessing everything (6:8–10). Paralleling a positive term with a negative one, Paul suddenly breaks the pattern in the phrase "dying, and yet *behold* we live" (6:9 RSV), taking the readers by surprise, shocking them awake to keep considering the rest of the list. He breaks verse nine's linguistic pattern of particle–participle–adversative conjunction–participle, with the particle and the finite verb, literally, "as dying and yet *behold we live*."

Paul's powerful proclamation is his own example of the living, life-giving God in action. The Corinthians would be reminded immediately of the preceding promise in 2 Corinthians 4:1–10 where they were told that carrying Jesus' death results in the revelation of Jesus' life. The break in parallelism mirrors Paul's and now his readers' astonishment: "We think we die—and yet—behold! we live."

Paul's effective use of ellipsis, anaphora, asyndeton, chiastic structure, periodically punctured parallelism—all woven together expound the exhaustive list of what he has suffered for the Corinthians and what that suffering means. It comes to a surprising and dramatic appeal in verse 11. Not until then does Paul's prose reach any satisfaction. Literally the passage reads:

> Our mouth (is) opened to you, Corinthians,
> our hearts (are) enlarged;
> you are not restricted in us,
> but you are restricted in your own affections;
> by the same exchange,
> as to children I speak,
> enlarge also yours.

Here and now is where and when Paul indicates the action that he wants the Corinthians to perform. His appeal returns to complete the earlier challenge, "Behold now (is) a welcomed time, behold now (is) a day of salvation" (6:2). Since he has explained fully and in the most satisfying form of written presentation how he and his associates have commended themselves to the Corinthians as authentic ministers, the Corinthians must now respond by welcoming Paul and his team as their authentic leaders.

2. Reason 2: The Corinthians Need to be Purified (6:14–7:3).

At this point occurs a passage that has baffled New Testament scholars. So odd does it appear to many that Paul should suddenly swing into a discussion of being "unequally yoked" (KJV) in 6:14 to 7:1, only to return to the identical phrasing about "making room" in the Corinthians' "hearts" in 7:2, that some have concluded that the passage must have not been intended by Paul to be here at all. Some think a later unknown editor of 2 Corinthians simply rammed it in—perhaps a piece of papyrus got mislaid from another codex, an early book of sewed-together pages, and was shuffled into the deck and passed on. Some do not believe that Paul even wrote the passage. They point to all the new words that are present, though new words abound in Paul, often appearing and never being repeated. (The apostle commanded a wide and varied vocabulary in several languages.) Finally, some conclude that indeed the passage is by Paul, but it is a reworking of some other piece of tradition that Paul has had on his mind and while pausing remembers it and thinks, "Say, why don't I put that piece in about not being unequally yoked before I forget it?"

Scholars making all of these conclusions have, we believe, not been following Paul's argument carefully enough. What looks to them like a passage on marriage (though the term is never used), haphazardly inserted in the text, interrupting the flow is actually the second half of Paul's proof for his case for acceptance. It is the necessary follow-through of the parallel threads we detailed in our opening commentary on this chapter. Paul, having established his claims and having pleaded for the Corinthians' understanding and acceptance, now addresses the rival claims to his. Such a movement from one side of the argument, Paul's claims and appeal—to the other, a refutation of his rivals' claims and a warning against them—is not unique to this passage. As we have shown, it forms the thread of the entire preceding half of the epistle. Like a great chiasm, Paul focuses the center of his argument in the entire book in this central contrasting of his and his rivals' claims. Having quoted a line from Greek poet Menander's comedy, *Thais*, "Bad company corrupts good character," he has previously warned the Corinthians (1 Cor. 15:33). In a like manner he attacks the bond between the Corinthians and his own accusers before he returns to restate his plea, reason number two having been now delivered. Verses 6:14–7:1 are not merely an aside by Paul or an insertion by an editor. They are a necessary part of Paul's argument. Paul is attacking all his rivals in one mighty slash: Do not be aligned with (1) pagans, (2) non-Christian Jews, (3) "superapostle" apostates, and, of course, an application can be made to marriage, for the Corinthians' flabby purity is always present in Paul's mind (e.g., 12:21).

The correlation of loyalty to God with loyalty to spouse is fundamentally ingrained in the Holy Scriptures from the first words of the prophets throughout the recorded ministry of Jesus into the early church. For God the new Israel is a spouse, a bride in robes purified and glittering with the good deeds of the saints (Rev. 19:8); and to God, apostasy is adultery, plainly and simply. Rejecting Paul, God's ambassador, is not only a crime against the reign of God, Paul's Commander-in-Chief, it is a familial sin against a family member, be he in the image of the Corinthians' spiritual father (his rejection being a subliminal form of imaged patricide) or rejected lover. The argument could be displayed in the following abbreviated schema:

6:1–2	Now is the day to act on God's grace
6:3–10	Paul's claims proved by his suffering
6:11–13	The request
6:14–7:1	Paul's warning not to accept rival partnerships
7:2–4	The request
7:5	Paul's claims re-echoed (in synopsis)
7:6–13	The Confirmation: Titus confirms that the Corinthians' response to Paul's letter means they intend to obey Paul's requests.

What Paul is summoning the Corinthians to recall is that they are not a marketplace where apostles of profit come to hawk their oratorical wares, but they together with Paul and his coworkers are the unified and holy temple of the living God.

In the history of Israel four temples were built. The first, by Moses about the year 1500 B.C., was a moveable temple. What is interesting is that its primary design was not to be a place of worship. As God ordered Moses in Exodus 25:8, "And let them make me a sanctuary, that I may dwell in their midst" (RSV), the primary purpose was to provide a place where God dwells. The concept became so ingrained in the Hebrews that God and God's emissaries had to counteract it to keep Israel from thinking God *only* lived in the temple (2 Chron. 2:6; 1 Kings 8:27; Isa. 66:1; Jer. 23:24). Worship became synonymous with entering the temple because when one comes into the presence of God, one worships.

The "tent of meeting" as it was called or the tabernacle had three basic sections: a court where the altar for burnt offerings stood; a holy place where the altar of incense stood; and the most holy place, the holy of holies, where the ten commandments, God's first written word, rested in the ark of the covenant beneath the mercy seat. The Spirit of God would descend like a cloud, the mysterious "Cloud of Unknowing" of the mystics, and envelop the tabernacle. Then God would be present to meet with Aaron, Moses' brother. God's presence made the holy place so terrible that if a bell did not announce the entrance of the high priest, Aaron would be struck dead. The inner holy of holies where God was most present could be entered only once a year on Yom Kippur, the Day of Atonement, after an elaborate service of purification. God's presence was so holy it was like a fire, purifying everything that entered his presence, instantly consuming anything impure.

When Christ died in our stead, his sacrificial death purified every human. Therefore the temple curtain to the holy of holies was ripped in two from top to bottom (Matt. 27:51). This signified that God's Spirit no longer dwelt in that place nor met God's people within the temple. God's Spirit rushed out into what was newly purified, and the people of God, the new Israel, became the moveable tent. This concept is heightened when we notice what words are employed by Paul to explain this truth. Greek has two words that are translated "temple." The first, *hieron*, signifies the whole temple, all the buildings, all the grounds, the balconies and the courts. But this is not the word Paul employs in 2 Corinthians 6:16. *Naos* (the closest English word we have for it is "sanctuary") was the holy place and the inner holy of holies. This is the word Paul uses to describe what God has made out of the Corinthians together with Paul and his ministering team: "For we are the sanctuary of the living God." God has not merely made them the tent or the temple but the holy of holies! The implications are staggering. God has not simply made a new stationary meeting place for Christians. One advantage of a tent over a temple is that it is moveable, but how much more moveable are a people! Wherever Christians go, God goes. And we have the privilege to represent God's most holy presence.

This passage is not the first time Paul has reminded the Corinthians of this fact. In 1 Corinthians 3:16 he wrote to them, "Don't you know that you yourselves are God's temple and that God's Spirit lives in you?" For this reason Paul was ferocious in admonishing them about their divisions. Since divisions destroy God's temple, Paul's warnings must be harsh in 1 Corinthians 3:17: "If anyone destroys God's temple, God will destroy him; for God's temple is sacred, and you are that temple." Therefore, even one immoral person among the holy people, the church, affects the entire structure. Thus Paul warns in 1 Corinthians 6:15: "Do you not know that your bodies are members of Christ himself? Shall I then take the members of Christ and unite them with a prostitute? Never!" This passage is particularly relevant for Corinth, where sexual immorality and pagan apostasy were so melded together. Like a spiritual form of AIDS, pollution enters both the body and the spirit through immorality, destroying the spirit and the body and beyond that destroying God's very meeting place with the people of God. Verse 19 continues: "Do you not know that your body is a temple of the Holy Spirit, who is in you, whom you have received from God?" The "you" is not singular but plural. And again the word for temple is *naos*. One sin by one Christian affects the very sanctuary of God, affecting not a building and not just simply that one individual but all Christians, all of the pillars, the living stones that comprise God's church and that are laid upon the chief cornerstone Christ. Therefore we, as the Corinthians, need to be very careful how we act. We are our brothers' and sisters' keepers, and what we do seriously affects them. For these reasons churches must discipline in love for the body's sake any individual who is immoral or divisive.

Today we spend a lot of money on making our church buildings lovely. We are good stewards of our facilities because we want to keep "the house of God" in good order. Once while meeting with other pastors in an urban church building that had been on the verge of closing until a congregation leased it, we heard the new pastor say, "The temple of God was in a shameful condition when we came." How many times as a little boy one of the present authors was pulled up sharply by a passing deacon and admonished, "Don't run in God's house, it's disrespectful!" Indeed, if we were still living in ancient Israel before Jesus became our sacrificial lamb once and for all history, we might spend all our money on our church building to make it beautiful. No one would enter without being purified. We would have detailed rules of conduct for anyone entering the church building. Only the holiest of elders would come to the holiest part and only very rarely and very carefully. Today, after Christ's death and resurrection, these rules are now turned around and applied to God's people, God's new dwelling.

For this reason we donate to a multitude of Christian relief organizations helping starving Christians and starving potential Christians worldwide. For this reason, also, we must be united with all true believers of all truly orthodox denominations, not quarreling, but letting the different church polities simply be different expressions of one united Church Triumphant. Therefore, not even one of us at one time should lapse and be immoral. We must treat one another in the same way the Hebrews were taught to treat the holy of holies. If we destroy even the least of our brothers and sisters, lead any astray by our immoral acts, we have destroyed God's temple, and God promises that we in turn will be destroyed. Thus says the Lord, in Isaiah 66:1–2: " 'Heaven is my throne and the earth is my footstool; what is the house which you would build for me, and what is the place of my rest? All these things my hand has made, and so all these things are mine,' says the Lord. 'But this is the person to whom I will look, the one that is humble and contrite in spirit, and trembles at my word' " (RSV). Like the Corinthians we have reason both to tremble and rejoice. John was struck by a mighty vision and a loud voice roaring that the dwelling of God is with people (Rev. 21:3). Since God has chosen to dwell in us, the way we treat other people, God's living tent, is of dire responsibility. No less than our own relationship with God and our continued existence hang upon it!

Eusebius, the great church historian from the 300s, knew this truth well when he pointed out that while Christians for two hundred years of persecution were not able to build temples, nevertheless God had a temple. Some of the saints God walled around as an "outer enclosure," a protective barrier. Unwavering faith was enough for them to serve in this capacity. To some who were stronger, God entrusted the entrances to the church proper. These were the evangelists who helped guide people entering. Then some were underprops of the first quadrangle (these were those being instructed in the gospels). Then as Christians became more and more learned in the Gospel and the Scriptures, they became supports holding up more and more of the church's structure. In this way God: "is constructing out of them all a great and kingly house, glowing and full of light within and without, in that not only their heart and mind, but their body too, has been gloriously enriched with the many-blossomed adornment of chastity and temperance" (Eusebius, *History of the Church* 10:4).

To Paul, the Christians at Corinth were like a building that belongs to God and on which Paul, Apollos, and the other coworkers were laboring. As Christ's construction workers, Paul laid the foundation and Apollos built upon it. This building, Paul points out again and again, is a temple. Building in stones of false believers, pagan prostitutes, dissension, breaks it down. Unyoking from Paul and from other true believers is splitting stones apart, a foolish act that threatens to topple the entire building down upon the Corinthians' heads, crushing and destroying their relationship with God. Rather, they should make in their own hearts room where love for Paul and for Paul's God can dwell. They should be using their time and energy in constructive ways; that is, ways that help construct the temple of God. How can they do this? Concrete ways to cement their relationship with Paul and with their fellow stones in the living temple are to resolve their own disagreements, and to be obedient to Paul and to their own promise to take up a temple offering to benefit their starving sisters and brothers, thus contributing to the collection Paul has been led to gather for Jerusalem.

B. Paul Has Confidence in the Corinthians (7:4–9:15)

1. Corinthians Repented Because of Paul's Letter (7:4–16).

As we have seen in the outlined argument of 6:1–7:13 that we traced in the previous section, Paul discerns that, in Titus's confirmation, the struggle for the Corinthians' obedience has entered a new stage. The Corinthians' response to Paul's recent letter shows their zeal and affection for Paul, Titus, and the other coworkers. This action encourages Paul so that he can go on to ask for their contribution (chs. 8–9) and later, their loyalty (chs. 10–13). Paul did mention having sent a previous letter in 2:4, probably the same prior letter to which he now refers. (See our comments in Chapter 2, Section B:2 on whether it is 1 Corinthians, a lost letter, or 2 Corinthians 10–13.)

According to the information in 2:1–11 and 7:4–16, Paul asked the Corinthians to change their behavior ("repent" 7:9) and to discipline someone, which they did! Therefore, they were "innocent in the matter" (7:11). Paul is discreet in concealing the exact problem in 2 Corinthians, which is a thoughtful action for the disputing parties but makes a reconstruction of the problem difficult for later curious readers. Nevertheless, this display of concern by the Corinthians shows that Paul has a reason for hope and confidence in them. The response has demonstrated that the Corinthians do have some love for Paul and his coworkers, which will be tested in the more difficult requests to come.

2. Corinthians Desired to Donate (8:1–9:15).

Now Paul brings his exhortation pointedly to a monetary level. Chapters 8 and 9 comprise what could be called in effect "Paul's Stewardship Sermon." Paul holds up the example of the poorer Macedonian churches before the materially comfortable Achaians weaving example, proverb, and plea together, alluding to past promises, present services, and to God's great and generous gift of Jesus, to encourage the Corinthians to give their portion to the accumulated gift of all the Greek churches. At risk is nothing less than Paul's own relationship with the churches, and by implication, the Corinthians' own salvation. Refusal would signify a rejection of Paul, Paul's gospel, partnership with the other churches in the body of Christ and acceptance of rival apostate apostles, their false blinded gospel, and a slipping back into a sub-Christian Judeo-paganism. The stakes are clearly more than money. But money, symbolic as it is of security and what one must truly value more than security when it is expended, serves as a concrete indication of where the Corinthians' loyalty stands. One votes with one's purse, and now Paul campaigns for that vote not simply on his own behalf, for the money is not for his benefit, but on behalf of Christ's church.

Paul's argument develops three questions in chapter 8 and chapter 9: Why should the Corinthians give? How should they give? How much should they give?

a. Why Should They Give? (8:1–9:15) This question is answered when Paul holds up the example of the Macedonian churches. Macedonia's donation came from its members' overflowing of sheer joy in God's grace (8:2), a desire to share in Paul's ministry (8:4), and at God's will (8:5). All of these reasons fit poignantly into the upbuilding of God's temple.

What the Macedonians have learned is that when one trades with God fairly, one is enriched. We have all heard the saying, "You don't get rich by giving it away." This appears to have been the attitude of the Corinthians. But the Macedonians' life of faith in God's grace, joy, and will had taught them a deeper truth. Proverbs 3:9–10 counsels, "Honor the Lord with your wealth, with the firstfruits of all your crops; then your barns will be filled to overflowing, and your vats will brim over with new wine." Hoarding one's money and property, as the rich fool in Luke 12 learned posthumously, is the very worst thing a believer can do. "You don't get rich by giving it away" is simply not true. A Christian does become rich by giving it away. Proverbs 11:24–25 points out, "One man gives freely, yet gains even more; another withholds unduly, but comes to poverty. A generous man will prosper; he who refreshes others will himself be refreshed."

For this reason God told the Israelites in Malachi 3:10, "'Bring the whole tithe into the storehouse, that there may be food in my house. Test me in this,' says the Lord Almighty, 'and see if I will not throw open the floodgates of heaven and pour out so much blessing that you will not have room enough for it.'" The Macedonians acted upon these truths, and from their deep poverty within testing troubles they overflowed with generosity in obedience to God and in partnership with Paul.

The Corinthians, Paul assumes, have a thorough knowledge of business success. Those who had been in the synagogue would know the Old Testament's view that God rewards liberality in giving. Paul assumes these factors and he also assumes that the Corinthians will honor the first gesture they made a year previously in giving and their promises to continue giving in the present year (8:10–12).

What Paul calls the Corinthians to do is to enter into a covenant of economic interdependence with the other Christian churches. He assures them that he does not want to make them poor and others rich but to make them equal with others (8:14), giving when in surplus and receiving when in need. Such a symbiotic relationship may have seemed superfluous to the currently successful nouveau-riche Corinthians, but as we saw in our foreground discussion in chapter 1, within twenty years of Paul's letter an earthquake would reduce them from givers to recipients. Thus Paul, acting on these assumptions and a hopeful trust in the good will of the Corinthians' promise, sends Titus, his trusted coworker, with a team to make the collection.

On one of Paul's visits to Jerusalem an uncircumcised Greek named Titus accompanied him (Gal. 2:1–3). Titus had come with Paul and Barnabas to Jerusalem from Antioch, either during the relief visit recorded in Acts 11:30 and 12:25, or the Jerusalem Council visit of Acts 15:2ff. If he came on this latter visit, Titus may have been a delegate of the uncircumcised brethren to the Jerusalem council, one of the "other believers" appointed to accompany Paul and Barnabas. In either instance, he left Antioch for Jerusalem with Paul and Barnabas and became one of their evangelism team.

The ministry of Titus we see developed into one of follow-through support. Paul placed him at various churches for various tasks. The bond between this Gentile believer and his Jewish leader became so strong, Paul loving his coworker Titus so dearly, that 2 Corinthians 2:13 tells us Paul refused an open door the Lord created at Troas to hasten to Macedonia in search of Titus. In this time of persecution, the welfare of other Christians counted above every other ministry for Paul—a startling attitude that all of us should keep in mind. Paul's first priority after God was people. His ministry was clearly people-oriented not empire building, for God rules already.

Comforted by Titus's well being, Paul and Timothy in 2 Corinthians 7:7 learn about the Corinthian response to Paul's letter (either 1 Corinthians or a missing letter) and his mind, like Titus's mind, is put at rest. Now Titus welcomes Paul's appeal (2 Cor. 8:6), enthusiastically going on his own accord to set up the collection at Corinth in company with two other "brothers." These are unnamed, but some speculate they could be Luke, Barnabas, or some other minister well known among the churches. As for Titus, Paul calls him no less than *koinōnos*, partner, and *sunergos*, coworker (a term of great respect and affection as we saw in our Timothy summary [2 Cor. 8:23]). Not simply a lackey of Paul, Titus is "urged" not "sent" according to 2 Corinthians 12:18, and Paul could assume that Titus was non-exploitive among the suspiciously sensitive Corinthians.

Paul abounds with affection when he writes of Titus. In the letter to Titus 1:4 he calls him his "true child" (RSV). Trusting him implicitly, Paul placed Titus as caretaker of several churches. He left him at Crete to straighten out what was defective, and to appoint elders. There Titus had to silence the circumcision party (Titus 1:10–12), an explosive task for a Gentile Christian who may once have been a second class Gentile Godfearer at the synagogue of Antioch. As Paul's emissary, Titus was urged to teach what befits sound doctrine (Titus 2:1), instructing everyone from the older men and women down to the youth. Titus himself had to show the example of "integrity, seriousness and soundness of speech" (2:7–8), a task Paul felt confident that Titus could handle. Paul invested him with God's authority to speak, exhort, and reprove, reminding the Cretans to be obedient to whatever is good (2:15; 3:1).

Task after task was given by Paul to Titus. In Titus 3:12–13 Paul begs him to come to Nicopolis after outfitting the famous Apollos and Zenas, a lawyer, and the very last we hear of him is that he has accompanied Paul to Rome and then left for Dalmatia, an area comprising present-day Albania and a part of Yugoslavia. The early church esteemed Titus, and Eusebius called him the first bishop appointed to the churches of Crete (Eusebius, *History of the Church* 3:4).

Now Paul continues his stewardship sermon by appealing to the Corinthians' own sense of honor. Employing the positive reinforcement we use with our own children ("Daddy and Mommy are very proud of you for saving up that money and taking it right up front and giving it to the deacons for the church's foster child in . . . ") Paul appeals in a passage full of pathos to the Corinthians' and his own reputation in the opinion of the Macedonians. Paul had obviously used the Corinthians' example of willingness to give the prior year to spur on the Macedonians. Since the results were even more than he had anticipated (8:2), now he turns and uses the Macedonians' example to the Corinthians. He initiates a healthy competition among the churches, each striving to outdo the others in acts of kindness and generosity. Truly they are like children, doing good for perhaps less than pure motivations, wanting to be thought well of; yet when any of us fallen humans examine our motivations, we always find them wanting against God's pure love. Paul is forming positive habits in the churches. Like a good teacher he is creating a team identity with mutual support against a common enemy—want! Through this he enables a true familial perspective, breaking each church out of its own myopia, expanding its vision to include its sister churches partnered within each church's own self-identity.

The Corinthians periodically catch fire from Paul's enthusiasm and glow for a time with generosity as they did the previous year, but without his presence to keep them inflamed they slip back into their natural parsimony. As a result Paul appeals to something less than pure, but a strong motivator that he can use toward good, their acute sense of business. Obviously realizing that his tactic could be construed as manipulative, he begins by cautioning the Corinthians that they should not feel forced to give: "Each should give what he has decided in his heart to give, not reluctantly or under compulsion, for God loves a cheerful giver" (9:7). Paul has already told them in verse 5 that he does not want their donation to be one "grudgingly given." To appeal to them and shore up their faltering resolve he makes the following statement, "The point is this: the one sowing sparingly, sparingly also reaps, and the one sowing bountifully, bountifully also reaps." The construction is almost a perfect parallelism, reflecting cause and effect in equal proportions. The way you act toward others rebounds to you. He does this by juxtaposing two adverbs "sparingly" and "bountifully" in both sides of his propositions.

While we are considering the words Paul chooses to express his thoughts, we should note the word choice for gift or donation is a fascinating one. It is *eulogia* (9:5), which denotes blessing, praise, or bountiful gift. Thus, 9:6 is a play on words. If the Corinthians give a bountiful gift, they will be rewarded bountifully. A great gift to others then becomes eventually a great gift to oneself. If the Corinthians give to the poor, they will not become impoverished. Certainly they will have a spiritual reward and they will feel emotionally good, too. But do these facets exhaust the reward Paul is promising? What kind of wealth is he alluding to here, metaphorical-spiritual wealth or literal? Obviously, the Proverbs and Malachi passages cited earlier promise literal material wealth. Does Paul mean this? The Corinthians, we must remember, already had sufficient for their current needs. Yet very soon they, too, would need to turn to other churches for aid. Paul might not have known that, but his interweaving of the material with the spiritual must have meant that he had both these levels of reward in mind. Paul did not separate the spirit and body as the later platonizing Christians in the Middle Ages came to do. Paul was concerned about the whole person, but not that the churches wallow in spirit-slaying luxury. God does not intend that. God intends that no Christian be in need. Toward this end God gave us one another. Moderation is always the Christian rule.

God's intentions hover over this entire discussion. In 9:8–9 Paul brings God directly into the argument, emphasizing that God is "able." Verse 9:10 accentuates the ability of God by describing God in a very lengthy subject as "The one furnishing seed to the sower and bread for food." The Corinthians need not worry that they will have enough "seed," for their current riches to God are like seed corn that needs to be scattered far and wide in generous measure. Planting peanuts in our garden, we learned the farmer's creed: three peanuts are planted—one for God, one for the birds, and one to grow. From one-third of the seed planted flourishes many peanuts. Living in thrifty New England, we were appalled to learn that we were supposed to pinch out a good deal of our tiny carrot plants that we had sown so generously. Reluctant to do so, we found none of them could grow into a thriving plant while they all huddled together, competing for nourishment. In like manner, extra wealth becomes a blockage. While surplus wealth could be out enriching someone else it becomes a burden on its keeper, dragging that one down with worry for its safety, keeping the owner's eyes earthward and stunting spiritual growth. But good business sages know that "the more you speculate, the more you accumulate," that is, "the one sowing bountifully, bountifully reaps." In this way, everybody wins: Everybody is enriched and is enriching one another. Our real fortunes are our Christian family and the God who is at its head. This God is all powerful, the one furnishing all seed. All of us can rely on the ultimate source of all wealth.

What will God do? Verse 9:8 tells us God will increase every grace. "Grace" (the word *charis*), means favor, gift. Our ability to give will increase, and 9:10 promises that God will supply and increase our "seed" as well as increase the harvest of our righteousness. Self-reliance, such a compelling temptation for "rugged individualist" North Americans, was an equal temptation for former pagans in Paul's day. *Autarkeia*, the word translated "what one needs" in the NIV in the phrase "having all that you need," was a favorite virtue of the Stoics and Cynics. As Bauer's *Lexicon* notes, it was "the state of one who supports himself without aid from others." Paul has drawn a kind of humorous paradox here: the Corinthians' great self-sufficiency allows them to give more to others. Thus, God will continue to keep them self-sufficient so that they can give sufficiently to others. The interlocking relationship to God and one's neighbor is assumed even if not recognized.

What separates this from a theology of greediness is that while God does return material benefits for material generosity, a lack of wealth such as the Macedonians had does not mean a lack of spirituality. As we see in the Corinthians' case, presence of wealth is not a sign of spirituality. All wealth does not come because people are generous, nor does spirituality only come from giving. Riches are not an end in themselves, for God is the great source of riches. They are provided to give an ability, and thus they create a responsibility: to give. God promises only to supply our needs, and God likes to do that through humans, one to another, alternating as the giver and receiver. Abundance is worthwhile to God in this way: it has a potential to increase a giver's spiritual strength.

But Jesus considered riches an afterthought. In Luke 12:28–31 he promised that if believers sought first the reign of God, food, drink, and shelter would be theirs as well. Treasures were to be stored up in heaven, attached to God who is our only true security (Luke 12:32–34). God's intention for material abundance, then, is periodically to give us enough for our needs and to give away. At other times God lets us have needs so that others may give back to us. Psalm 112:9 corroborates this idea, pointing out that people who truly fear the Lord by scattering abroad gifts to the poor thereby increase their own personal righteousness. Generosity, thus, has three results: it increases one's own righteousness; supplies needs of others thereby demonstrating our love for them (8:2), and gives thanks to God (9:10–11). It is also a holy act in that it mirrors God's own generosity in giving the one great sacrificial gift of Jesus (9:15). To the Corinthians, who already considered themselves rich in knowledge, Paul was demonstrating a new type of enrichment, a surpassing one (9:11, 14).

A further dimension comes when we realize the word employed for donation in 9:13 is *homologia*, confession, agreement, vow (pledge). Some translations like the NIV go as far as to translate the word "confession." How can a donation be a confession? One gives because one trusts God. Giving is an act of faith. That is why God was given the firstfruits in Proverbs 3:9–10. Giving is a sign of trust that God will make other fruits follow to supply our needs, and God rewards that faith. Interestingly, a bank account, cupboard, or storehouse is mentioned in various passages we have cited. In Luke 12:16–21, the rich fool builds storehouses to feel more secure in years to come. In Proverbs the people who give to the Lord do end up with the filled storehouses the rich fool sought, but they are permitted by God to enjoy them. In Malachi the Lord tells the people that if they give to God's storehouses their own production will greatly increase. The difference is in the question: Was the storehouse or bank account accrued before or after obeying God? Does the person trust in God or the First National? Is wealth a goal or a side benefit?

So, why should we give? If we trade with the Lord, we will always gain. But we will never have enough unless we give it away. We should put our trust in the Lord, for who is more trustworthy? If we put God to the test by acting on our faith we will not be disappointed.

b. How Achaians Should Give (8:1–9:15). Paul despite his urging is not some telephone-type, high pressure button-holer, sweeping in on the Corinthians, stirring up their guilt, shaking their resolve, and catching the denarii as they tumble down. Verses 10–11 of chapter 8 tell us that his current appeal was part of a program of planned giving he had initiated a year earlier. At that time he had taken apparently minimal donations, preferring to collect the balance after the Corinthians had had ample opportunity to pray, consider, and plan. Now he simply wanted them to fulfill the promises they had made, not eschewing any gift, but simply stressing that the willingness is what counts and the amount is never too small if it is truly dictated by what one has.

Paul's program is well worth considering today when we are continually in danger of being conditioned to give to whatever appeal is the most manipulative. Christians should not always have to give on the spot to maintain their reputations. Paul took a year to collect from Corinth for a prophesied famine. The point is that the Corinthians must give, but the timetable should be orderly. There are times when a quick donation is crucial, but these are not regular occurrences. Regular tithing ought to stave off a number of crisis situations and help our brothers and sisters to live in tranquility as we hope to do. The important thing is that the Corinthians fulfill their obligations, keep their word (8:24). Paul's goal is not for them to feel forced, but for them to decide in their hearts so that they do not give with regret (pain) that their giving is not under compulsion (9:5–7).

Why is Paul concerned about this issue? Because "God loves a cheerful giver" (9:7). Why does God love cheerful givers? Verse 8 implies the answer: because a cheerful giver trusts in God. The giver is cheerful because he or she is expecting good things to come.

One danger here is that foolish Christians might decide not to give because they are not cheerful about giving. While we should not let others force us to give, some of us need to act, to take a chance by putting our much loved security into God's hands before we can fully trust God and experience the relief of cheerful feelings. If God does not love our way of giving, that fact does not mean we should cease giving entirely. We need to keep working on our attitudes. We can trust the God who searches our hearts to honor our intentions despite our sinful failings. Attitudes will follow actions. We act as the Christians we want ourselves to become, and we will become them.

So how were the Corinthians to give? Paul shows by example that they were to plan ahead. Then they needed to be certain to fulfill the promises made in their plans. And finally they were to do this freely, trusting in God whose blessings fill the heart with joy.

c. How Much Should They Give? (8:1–9:15) No doubt this is the part of the sermon the Corinthians were listening for. One can picture them huddled on their daises, some of them perhaps slipping into fetal curls, pulling their purple robes tighter around them, eyes narrowed, ears perked for the bottom line. Paul must have anticipated such an attitude, for he moves to the bottom line almost immediately, figuring probably that little else he had to say would be digested by the Corinthians while they were straining to hear what the bill was going to cost. Therefore, he opens in 8:1–5 with the example of the poor Macedonians' generosity; sanctions Titus as the one to collect from the Corinthians; and in verses 6–9 urges them to adopt giving as a virtue, a sign of sincerity, and a tribute to the sacrificially giving Lord Christ. Then he immediately moves to a discussion of amount (10ff.). More will follow in his sermon, much more, and even the amount will appear again in 9:7. But Paul must have known the stingy Corinthians would hear little until they heard how much, so he tells them, "For if the willingness is there, the gift is acceptable according to what one has, not according to what he does not have" (8:12). In other words, "Do not feel guilty for what you do not have to give. Equality with others (*isotēs*, 8:13) is the goal, not relief for one and trouble for another."

Missionaries, who are the most self giving of people, sometimes die gloriously, sacrificing their last bit of nourishment for others. This is a special Christ-like act between God and the doer, but it is not the regular program of ministry Paul calls upon Christians to fulfill. Otherwise we would all look like IRA prisoners on a hunger strike. As 8:13–15 reveals, God's master plan in giving is to create a symbiotic family, each part looking out for the other, relief flowing back and forth in love according to need. Some Christians are so proud they will not accept help from anyone, thinking there is some kind of special virtue in this attitude. All that this self-sufficiency does is stunt the growth of the rest of the body by not letting it exercise its gifts of generosity and thereby grow spiritually.

Ultimately, this sort of sacrifice is selfish. Its goal becomes paternalistic or maternalistic—one side always gives, the other side always receives. Such an end violates God's master plan. Therefore, we should take cardinal care that we do not keep more than our share of the world's goods. By doing so we weaken the reciprocal nature of God's community. We need instead to be immediately passing goods on to brothers and sisters in need, being ready ourselves to receive from God's great cooperative bank of the saints when we stand in need. And we do not need to feel guilty for what we cannot give, if we truly are giving what we can.

Finally, the Corinthians and we are lectured that we cannot outdo our Lord Jesus. The Lord always goes one step further. In giving Jesus gave up riches to become poor so that by his poverty we might become rich (8:9). Jesus, who is not equal with us but our master, went beyond equality with us to great sacrifice to ensure that we would be equal with each other. How could the Corinthians—how can we, reject so great a plea?

Therefore a stewardship sermon based on Paul's thought could be summarized as follows: Why give? The Lord is trustworthy, so trade with the Lord. You can only benefit. How should we give? Plan ahead when possible, fulfill your obligations, and freely give. How much should we give? One cannot give what one does not have. One should give proportionately, for the goal is equality with others, creating a reciprocal giving community. And above all these facets, Paul closes his discourse in gratitude to God for the indescribable gift of grace God first gave all of us (9:15).

For Further Study

1. Paul claims he has modeled his ministry after Christ's, not after Moses', in 3:7–18. In 2 Corinthians what are some of the ways Paul's ministry differs in following Christ instead of following Moses' example? Are there any similarities? As a Christian in your own life of witness in the church, at home, on

the job, in school, how can you model your ministering after Christ?

2. Paul wants the Corinthians to open their hearts to him and his coworkers in 6:13 and 7:2. In our churches how can we open our hearts to other Christians and other churches?

3. What does not being "unequally yoked" mean for you and your church?

4. How is your church like the living temple of God?

5. In light of the fact that the people of Christ are the temple of God, what should be our attitude toward our church buildings? What are their roles for us?

6. Eusebius drew a portrait of Christians as different pillars of the spiritual temple of Christ. What part do you think you have?

7. Paul and his coworkers built on the foundation laid by Christ. How are you yourself a construction worker for Christ?

8. Reviewing Paul's stewardship sermon: Why should you give? How should you give? How much should you give?

9. Do you believe a Christian gets rich in both spiritual and material things by giving riches away?

Chapter 5

Paul's Warning: Change or Be Disciplined
(2 Corinthians 10:1–13:11)

Paul ends chapter 9 with the exultant benediction, "Thanks be to God for his indescribable gift!" Paul expresses praise in the third major section of his letter (6:1–9:15) because he remembers the joy of meeting Titus in Macedonia (7:5–7) and the joy of remembering God's provisions for the faithful believer. Chapters 8 and 9 are especially written to the entire province of Achaia because in Paul's chronological schema he stands at the entrance to Achaia, the province immediately south of Macedonia from whence he writes.

In Chapter 10:1 he has entered into Corinth itself. Paul's mood dramatically changes as he confronts head-on the foes to whom he has alluded throughout—the opponents who have come to Corinth to undermine his whole ministry and the church that has welcomed these opponents. He stands now alone, without his coworkers, even as once before he entered Corinth alone (Acts 18:1–5), because he must challenge those people who falsely accuse him: "By the meekness and gentleness of Christ, I appeal to you—I, Paul, who am 'timid' when face to face with you, but 'bold' when away!" Paul first highlights how he and his coworkers do *not* act—in a worldly fashion (10:1–18). Then he highlights how they do work (11:1–12:18). Finally, he summarizes his defense (12:19–13:11).

A. Paul Defends His Team's Actions as Not Worldly (10:1–11:11)

Paul begins chapter 10 by highlighting *who* makes the exhortation: "Myself, I, Paul, I appeal." This appeal comes not

from any stranger but from the spiritual father who planted the
seed of the Corinthians' new birth (12:14; 1 Cor. 4:15). He
appeals to the Corinthians; he does not command. He appeals
through the midst of Christ's mildness and graciousness. Paul,
figuratively, stands between Christ's "meekness" and "gentleness" to make his appeal. Paul's appeal will never be effective
without Christ's "meekness" and "gentleness." "Meekness"
and "gentleness" are two synonyms that as a pleonasm therefore
emphasize one idea, humility.

"Meekness" (*praütēs*), the noun, and its adjective, "meek,"
occur only sixteen times in the New Testament, but wherever
they occur they are significant. Jesus said, "I am *gentle* and
humble in heart, and you will find rest for your souls."
Therefore, Jesus invites everyone who is weary and burdened to
enjoy Jesus' rest and to trust Jesus' yoke (Matt. 11:28–30).
Praütēs refers to mildness or gentleness. The adjective refers to
"mild, soft, gentle" things (as a soft voice), persons, actions, and
feelings. Jesus is the ox-driver who places the yoke on gently
and takes loving care of the oxen. Zechariah had prophesied that
Jerusalem's king would come, "*gentle* and riding on a donkey"
(9:9; Matt. 21:5). Mildness or "gentleness" is one of the fruits of
the Holy Spirit (Gal. 5:23). It is the way Christians should live
(Eph. 4:2; Col. 3:12; Titus 3:2). It describes the way to restore
someone "overtaken in a trespass" or to correct an opponent
(Gal. 6:1; 2 Tim. 2:25; 1 Peter 3:15). Wherever *praütēs* occurs,
"love" is never far away, as in 1 Corinthians 4:21 where a
"loving and *gentle* spirit" is contrasted with a "rod for whip-
ping."

The second attribute of Christ, "gentleness" (*epieikeia*), is
personified outside the New Testament as Clemency. *Epieikeia*
refers to reasonableness, fairness, and equity that is contrasted
at times with "righteousness" (*dikaiosunē* 5:21). It is the
opposite of the strict letter of the law. Paul uses *epieikeia* in
contrast to violence and quarrelsomeness. "Gentleness" or
"reasonableness" is a quality that an overseer should have
(1 Tim. 3:3; see also 1 Peter 2:18). Paul, in effect, says that his
appeal is through the gentleness that comes from love and the
gentleness that comes from reasonableness, all in Christ, who is
gentle.

Christ's "gentleness" ("meekness" and "reasonableness") is not the outflow of a fearful spirit, someone so scared or so compromised that he or she is "lukewarm" toward people or issues. Christ's "meekness" is the overflow of a loving spirit. It is the meekness or gentleness that comes from God's great *hesed* love, God's compassion. Paul has already told his readers about "the Father of compassion and the God of all comfort" (1:3). He has told them that their ministry comes "through God's mercy" (4:1). He has reminded them of "the grace of our Lord Jesus Christ, that though he was rich, yet for your sakes he became poor, so that you through his poverty might become rich" (8:9). Their gifts are "the proof" of their "love," that reaches out to others because of "the surpassing grace" God had given them (8:24; 9:14).

Paul makes his appeal on the basis of God's compassion, Christ's gentleness—not on the basis of God's justice, because God's justice has already been met by Christ becoming "sin for us" (5:21). The Corinthians have plenty of the world's critical spirit that welcomes leaders who in turn criticize and subjugate. Paul appeals through the double columns of "meekness" and "gentleness" because he wants the Corinthians to learn about these aspects of God's nature, aspects in their own characters they did not follow. Because they did not comprehend God's compassion, gentleness, and mildness, they therefore found Paul deficient because his aim was to be compassionate, gentle, mild; in other words, loving.

Who is this Paul in the sight of the Corinthians? He is the one who is "timid" (literally, "humble") when face to face with them, but "bold" when away! (10:1). Some people accused Paul and Timothy of living "by the standards of this world," literally "according to the flesh walking" (10:2). Paul already had discussed the Corinthians' complaint that his change of plans was "fleshly" (1:17). Paul is the one who seems "to be trying to frighten" them with his letters. Some say, "His letters are weighty and forceful, but in person he is unimpressive [literally, 'weak'] and his speaking amounts to nothing" (10:9–10). He does not love them since he refuses to accept a salary from them (11:7–11). To them Paul is lowly, fleshly, ungenuine, weak, ineffectual, and unloving. Paul's public esteem in a Gallup poll among the Corinthians at this time would have been very, very low!

Who are these "some people" who think Paul, Timothy, and possibly his other coworkers "live by the standards of this world"? Who are Paul's opponents at Corinth and what are they like? Let us take a few moments to arm ourselves with some information about them before we proceed with our examination of 10:1–10.

1. Paul's Opponents (10:10–12:13).

Next to the number of letters in 2 Corinthians, interpreters most disagree about the type of opponents Paul combated in Corinth and their relationship to opponents in other places.

In 1 Corinthians we see no definite overt indications of people visiting the Corinthians and inciting them to oppose Paul. While we see no external opponents, however, the difficulties Paul had with the Corinthians would create an environment conducive to agitation from outsiders who were opposed to Paul's message. For example, many of the Corinthians did not regard leaders in a proper manner. Instead they pitted leaders against each other in their imaginations and factionalized behind them (e.g., 1 Cor. 1:10–16; 3:4–9; 4:6–7, 16–18; 11:18). Paul complained that the Corinthians imputed to their leaders the same kind of divisions that they were having with each other, for example, at the Lord's Supper. So they pitted factions following Paul against factions following Apollos against factions following Christ. Since they did not perceive the interdependence among themselves, they did not perceive the interdependence among the team of leaders who ministered to them. Next they questioned Paul's apostleship (1 Cor. 4:3–4; 9:1–3). Further, they were worried that Paul and Barnabas were going to depend upon them financially (1 Cor. 9:6). Some were even questioning cardinal Christian doctrines: for example, "How can some of you say that there is no resurrection of the dead?" . . . (1 Cor. 15:12). Possibly because of all this divisiveness over leadership, Apollos did not now want to revisit Corinth ("I strongly urged [Apollos] to go to you with the brothers. He was quite unwilling to go now, but he will go when he has the opportunity," 1 Cor. 16:12).

Into this environment of hostility and division came Paul's accusers. Paul does not mention any external opponents until chapter 11 of 2 Corinthians. But when he does, he does so with great indignation. These opponents claimed they were better apostles than Paul: "I am [not] in the least inferior to these 'super- (from *huperlian*, an adverb meaning exceedingly, beyond measure, overmuch, preeminently) apostles'" (2 Cor. 11:5). This defense of Paul's is repeated again in 12:11. The super-apostles had an autocratic style (2 Cor. 11:20), according to Paul, making the Corinthians slaves (cf. 4:5; Gal. 2:4). They exploited the Corinthians, Paul using the word *katesthiō* (eating up, devouring, consuming) to describe them. They took advantage (the reference may be to hunting or fishing), catching the Corinthians unawares. They put on airs, *epairō* (meaning raising or uplifting oneself, acting haughtily), and struck the Corinthians in the face (2 Cor. 11:20). In Acts 23:1–5 we discover that only the high priest had the right to slap anyone in the face.

How did these outsiders get away with such outrages? They had impressive appearances and were skillful speakers. Paul in 11:6 has to defend himself against their accusations, pointing out that he may not have been professionally trained as a speaker, "unlearned in the word," but he has knowledge, and this knowledge has been demonstrated in "every way." Next, the unscrupulous opponents turn even Paul's demonstrations against him. His letters they say are heavy (from *barus*, heavy or burdensome and powerful), but "the presence of the body is weak and the word despised, or of no account" (10:10). Hans Dieter Betz has written a fine study of Paul's defense, contending that Paul's problems here are with rhetoricians or sophists not with philosophers.[1] Dionysius of Halicarnassus tells us that these rhetoricians/sophists whose focus was not philosophy but the art of persuasion entered in his generation (30–8 B.C.). As he saw it, "another Rhetoric stole in and took" the place of the old philosophic Rhetoric:

> intolerably shameless and histrionic, ill-bred and without a vestige either of philosophy or of any other aspect of liberal

[1] Hans Dieter Betz, "Paul's Apology: II Corinthians 10–13 and the Socratic Tradition," *The Center for Hermeneutical Studies in Hellenistic and Modern Culture*, Colloquy 2, 1970 (Berkeley: Center for Hermeneutical Studies, 1975).

education. Deceiving the mob and exploiting its ignorance, it not only came to enjoy greater wealth, luxury and splendour than the other, but actually made itself the key to civic honours and high office (The Ancient Orators 1).

But wise Jews like Philo saw through the emptiness of the rhetoricians/sophists' approach and praised the simplicity of clear speech when dealing with scriptural matters. For example, in *The Contemplative Life* Philo praised the President of the Essenes because:

> (when) he discusses some question arising in the Holy Scriptures . . . he has no thought of making a display, for he has no ambition to get a reputation for clever oratory but desires to gain a closer insight into some particular matters and having gained it not to withhold it selfishly from those who if not so clearsighted as he have at least a similar desire to learn. His instruction proceeds in a leisurely manner; he lingers over it and spins it out with repetitions, thus permanently imprinting the thoughts in the souls of the hearers (X:75–6).

Such was Paul's approach, and he, too, should have been praised for it, but the Corinthians were not wise and did not praise him; instead they listened to the scoffing of the verbally florid.

No doubt these rhetoricians went on to boast of special revelations from God. Perhaps this is why Paul counters with his own revelations by describing himself in the third person, thereby appearing more impartial and objective (12:1–5), and pointing up the arrogance of his opponents' self-inflated bragging.

Apparently Paul's opponents received money and led a more comfortable life than Paul and his coworkers led, for after Paul refutes the charges that he has been a financial burden on the Corinthians (11:7–11), he concludes in verse 12 that he wants to remove the basis of the claim of those who contend they work on the same terms that Paul and Timothy work. Paul can say he is a better servant than they are because he has had more misfortunes and almost died, something they have not done (11:23–27). A similar list of suffering can be found in 4:7–12 and 6:4–10. Philo has well described a teacher who puts on airs and financially exploits the student, a description that fits the super-apostles:

> Often on the other hand some teacher of the lower subjects, who has chanced to have a gifted pupil, boasts of his own teaching power, and supposes that his pupil's high attainments are due to him alone. So he stands on tiptoe, puffs himself out, perks up his neck and raises high his eyebrows, and in fact is filled with vanity, and demands huge fees from those who wish to attend his courses; but when he sees that their thirst for education is combined with poverty, he turns his back on them as though there were some treasures of wisdom which he alone has discovered. That is the condition called "having in the womb," a swollen, vanity-ridden condition, robed in a vesture of inordinate pride, which makes some people appear to dishonor virtue, the essentially honorable mistress in her own right of the lower branches of knowledge (Preliminary Studies XXIII: 127–28). Such false teachers were the super-apostles, full of vanity, disparaging loyalty, humility and other virtues, manipulating the Corinthians for financial gain.

Theologically these teachers were Jewish Christians who boasted of their Hebrew heritage particularly, no doubt, to the Gentile Christians among the Corinthians. So Paul must counter, "Are they Hebrews? So am I. Are they Israelites? So am I. Are they Abraham's descendants? So am I. Are they servants of Christ? . . . I am more" (11:22–23). Of what do these opponents boast?—their style of leadership, their language, descent, traditions, race. If they were only Christians, they would not brag of being Abraham's descendants. If they were only Jews, they would not boast of being servants of Christ. But to Paul they were servants of Satan, worshiping another Jesus, a different Spirit, another gospel (11:4). As Satan disguises himself as an angel of light, so are these disguised as apostles of Christ (11:13–15). Paul's analogy is aptly drawn. Thus, in summary, the external opponents in chapters 10–12 were characterized by their haughty consideration of themselves as being better apostles than Paul was. They had impressive appearances and wielded authority in an autocratic style. They spoke skillfully and boasted of special revelations from God, boasting of their Hebrew heritage and taking money from believers, insuring a more comfortable lifestyle than that of Paul and his coworkers. These opponents Paul considered heretical.

Summoning up such explicit identification suggests that other vaguer references in the epistle also apply to the false apostles. They may be the peddlers of God's word, retailing the gospel like merchants, provisioning the saints with spiritual food like tavern keepers (2:17). These are the ones who bear letters of recommendation (3:1), who falsify God's word, using trickery and cunning (4:2). Priding themselves in their own positions (5:12, 16; 10:12), they boast in another's labor (10:15–16; 11:12).

New Testament scholars have debated over the exact nature of the pseudo-apostles' false doctrine. Fedinand Christian Baur, an early German scholar (1792–1860), believed theirs was a Judaizing gospel, setting Peter up as a figurehead (e.g., 1 Cor. 1:12, the "Cephas party"), precipitating a lifelong battle between Paul and their conservative Jewish Christianity. While this position sheds much light on Paul's insistence on a gospel freed from law, developments took the ideas overboard claiming that only epistles that reflected this battle were genuine. C. K. Barrett and Johannes Munck have modified this position today.

Other scholars have seen a Gnostic element in Paul's opponents, a Jewish Gnosticism as Schlatter termed it. Irenaeus in his *Against Heresies* (ca. A.D. 180) gives us an early description of Christian Gnosticism. A syncretism of pagan thought with Christian belief, it posited that matter is evil (thus Gnostics could be either libertine or ascetic, both tendencies being present, as we have seen, in the Corinthians). Salvation is by knowledge, another weakness of Corinth, therefore neither atonement, nor moral behavior affects one's salvation. Salvation essentially is seen as escape from the corporeal world of matter. God is transcendent spirit and to God reach the disembodied souls of the chosen few. Only some humans contain within them the divine spark of life, imprisoned in their material bodies. Demons try to keep that spark unrecognized by the few. The universe itself emanates from God in numerous spheres of beings called aeons. One of these, Christ, liberates the few from confinement in the material body by giving them *gnōsis*, or knowledge, passwords that take the chosen few through the various levels of aeons in a heavenly ascent to God. While the few (in this case, the false apostles) gain knowledge easily, others called psychics must struggle (and pay) to get it. Carnals are those who cannot be saved, a class of humanity over whom both the few, called the pneumatics from the word *pneuma* (spirit), and the second level psychics can feel spiritually superior.

Some scholars such as Edwin M. Yamauchi in *Pre-Christian Gnosticism* argue historically that such an involved scheme only existed in the second century, while only a few pre-gnostic elements existed at the time Paul was combating the pseudo-apostles. These elements included astrology, an eastern idea that still plagues us today. Astrology claimed that the heavenly stars and planets control earthly events. The view was fatalistic since human destiny was thereby taken out of human hands. Philosophers such as the later Stoics and Platonists fostered it.

Platonic thought from Greece contributed the ideas that matter is evil (a belief incorporated in the early heresy called docetism [from the word "to seem"] asserting that Jesus only "seemed" to have a body and to die, a heresy John combats in 1 John)—that salvation comes from leaving the body and ascending to the stars—and that salvation is captured through knowledge. Stoics saw the soul as encrusted with a mud-like substance and needing to be liberated. Mystery religions fed in the idea of secret doctrines, available only to the chosen few initiates who gained secret knowledge. Often sexually-oriented, their secrets involved intercourse between the gods. And although they had myths of dying and resurrecting gods, there was no Redeemer God entering history as a human in their theologies before the second century.

Were Paul's opponents at Corinth Jewish Gnostics or of an incipient gnosticizing tendency? With a classical definition of Gnosticism, no. However, with a broad definition using the word "incipient" or pre- or proto-gnostic, one can posit a kind of infant Jewish Christian gnosticism as does Walter Schmithals in *Gnosticism in Corinth* . But though we see that the Corinthians emphasized knowledge, do we know that the super-apostles did? If so, Paul would have listed "puffed-up knowledge" or some such phrase along with their other failings that he attacked.

More information could be garnered on the opponents if we could establish that these opponents of the last four chapters of 2 Corinthians are the same as those in Philippians 3:2–11, in Galatians, and in Romans 16:17–20. At least we notice that they are similar. Acts seems to indicate a persistent Jewish movement within the Christian church to set Paul's and Peter's understandings of the gospel against each other (cf. Gal. 2:12). In Acts 11:1–3 a group from Jerusalem called the circumcision party (literally, "those out of circumcision") criticized Peter for eating and fraternizing with Gentiles. They were silenced when they heard of Peter's experience in Joppa (Acts 11:4–18). Again we see the same concerns voiced in the region of Judea and within Jerusalem (Acts 15:1–5). Further, the Jerusalem council decision to free believers from most of the legal regulations applied only to Gentiles. When Paul returned to Jerusalem before his imprisonment, James and the elders told him of thousands of Jews who had become Christians who were still zealous for the law and wanted their children circumcised (Acts 21:20–26).

Clearly there seemed to be a movement of Jewish Christians actively antagonistic to Paul's message and methods. Whether they followed Paul from city to city (as hostile Jews may have done from Antioch and Iconium in Acts 14:19) is speculatory. It may not be that the identical people appeared at every city, but there are many similarities between Paul's external opponents at Corinth, Philippi, Galatia, and those referred to in Romans. All were Jewish Christians who accentuated their Hebrew heritage. They had confidence in their earthly status (2 Cor. 11:18; Phil. 3:3). They did not emphasize the need to share Christ's sufferings (2 Cor. 11:23–33; 13:4; Phil. 3:10, 18; Gal. 6:12–13; Rom. 16:18). Paul considered them to be evil and deceitful and described them with strong negative adjectives (2 Cor. 11:4, 13–15; Phil. 3:2; Rom. 16:17–20).

In 2 Corinthians these believers accentuated dissensions, preaching and living out another gospel, tampering with God's word. Did that parallel those who stressed a need for circumcision and righteousness under the law in Phil. 3:2–9, or those in

Galatians 1:6; 2:12; 5:2–3? Were these the smooth talking flatterers who caused divisions, deceiving with contrary teaching and serving their own appetites in Romans 16:17–18? If so, they were potently effective, for even Barnabas under pressure weakened and joined Peter according to Galatians 2:13. Theirs was a renewed bondage (2:4; 5:1). Oscar Cullmann thinks that the Jewish-Gentile Christian controversies increased so severely in the latter half of the sixties that extremist Jewish Christians brought both Peter and Paul to their martyrdom by publicly accusing them.[2] Whether such a radical statement is true or not, the dissension among believers of different backgrounds raged shamefully in the infant church.

2. Words of Attack Become Words of Praise (10:1–11).

Paul again and again in this letter takes the accusations of his critics and reinterprets their slander as compliments of appropriate and laudable behavior for followers of the "meek and gentle" Christ.

Was Paul "timid" or "lowly" (10:1)? *Tapeinos*, the adjective, *tapeinōsis*, the noun, and *tapeinoō*, the verb, are from the same word family that metaphorically means lowly or humble. Literally, it means "low," not rising far from the ground, as in low regions or low in stature. Who calls himself "lowly"? *Jesus* is the one who is "gentle" (*praüs*) and "humble" (*tapeinos*) in heart (Matt. 11:29), even as the prophesied Messiah was to be humble (Isa. 53:8). Paul describes Jesus explicitly as a model for all believers in Philippians 2:1–11, the Jesus who "humbled himself." Mary describes herself as a "slave" with a "humble state" (*tapeinōsis*; Luke 1:48). In other words, she is poor without much power in her society. Jesus described the greatest person in God's reign as anyone who "humbles himself" (*tapeinoō*) like a little child, and welcomes such a little child in his name (Matt. 18:4–5). When Paul is accused of being too "lowly," he proceeds to describe throughout his letter a "lowly" leadership style.

Did some people reckon Paul and his associates as "walking

[2]Cullmann, Oscar, *Peter: Disciple—Apostle—Martyr: A Historical and Theological Study*, trans. Floyd V. Filson (Philadelphia: Westminster, 1953), pp. 89–109.

according to the flesh" (10:2)? Paul responds with the marvelous play on words: "in flesh walking not according to flesh fighting" (10:3). He keeps the noun "flesh" ("world" NIV) but introduces it with two contrasting prepositions "in" and "according to." Yes, they walk or live *in* the flesh. Paul does not see matter as evil or unreal. (See also 5:1–4.) In addition, Paul and his coworkers have certainly had difficulties in their ministry, in other words, they live "in the flesh." "Flesh" is in the first phrase a neutral word. But no, they do not fight or organize their life *according to* the flesh. The way they organize their ministry is not under the dominion or according to the rules of a world of sin.

Paul draws a sustained description of his ministry, using military terms that would appeal to the Corinthians, living as they did, in the capital of a province overrun with military personnel. Paul says that "we do not wage war" as the world does (10:3), but then he goes on to describe how they do "wage war" or battle or do military service. "The weapons of our warfare" are powerful enough to destroy "fortresses" (10:4). These weapons are powerful because they are acceptable to and empowered by God. The "fortresses" with which Paul has to deal are false arguments and reasonings—in other words, the false accusations against him and the false understandings of the Christian life. Another "fortress" is the "pretension that sets itself up against the knowledge of God" (10:5). "Pretension" literally is a "height, exaltation, stronghold." Paul may have had in his mind as he wrote these words the Acrocorinth, the fortified mountain that loomed 1,886 feet over ancient Corinth. The writer of 1 Maccabees used the same verb "set oneself up" to describe Philip and Perseus and others who "lifted up themselves" or attacked in battle the dominion of the Roman empire (8:5). Paul and his coworkers do wage a war, but it is a war against those people who have rejected the dominion of God. Consequently, when they are victorious, they, too, "take captive" or "carry prisoners" (10:5), but their prisoners are thoughts that must become subject to obedience to Christ, the proper Ruler. They are "ready to punish every act of disobedience," but they punish only when the Corinthian "obedience is complete" (10:6).

Similarly, Paul's warrior presence is considered by his

critics to be "weak." He quotes their complaint in 2 Corinthians 10:10 that his letters were terrifying, but he did not frighten when he visited in person. In this way they contrasted his "burdensome" and "powerful" letters, in which most likely they referred to the many injunctions and prohibitions Paul set down in such an authoritative manner or the effective and impressive writing style, with a bodily appearance whose unattractiveness might have been literal. Thus, they characterized him as being weak of bodily appearance with a speech amounting to nothing, despised and disdained. Ironically, Paul seems from 1 Corinthians to have worked consciously on having a speech "amounting to nothing." As he wrote:

> When I came to you, brothers, I did not come with eloquence or superior wisdom as I proclaimed to you the testimony about God. For I resolved to know nothing while I was with you except Jesus Christ and him crucified. I came to you in weakness and fear, and with much trembling. My message and my preaching were not with wise and persuasive words, but with a demonstration of the Spirit's power, so that your faith might not rest on men's wisdom, but on God's power (1 Cor. 2:1–5).

Obviously, these critics either did not have ears to comprehend Paul's message or had never read or heard Paul's manner of communication explained. Probably it differed from Apollos's manner, for Luke wrote of him, "He was a learned man [literally a man of words]" (Acts 18:24). Perhaps this was why some Corinthians proclaimed "I follow Apollos" and others reacted "I follow Paul" (1 Cor. 1:12). Perhaps, too, the super-apostles manifested glittering words of wisdom, backed by a powerful and burdensome bodily presence. Thus, weakness, *asthenēs* in 10:10, was intended to slander Paul, carrying with it negative connotations of one unimpressive and unauthoritative, to be ridiculed and ultimately ignored. But Paul, as we shall soon see, transformed the word into ringing compliment.

3. Measuring According to God's Canon (10:12–18).

Paul in the first part of chapter 10 explains that his team's warfare is not like a worldly warfare (10:1–6), that the accusations made against him are untrue (10:7–11). He then continues to argue that any boasting he does is not an untrue boasting in someone else's work (10:12–18).

Paul now uses a consistent imagery from the world of commerce and government—measurement. When anything is measured it needs some standard by which to measure. Originally "canon" (10:13, 15–16) came from the Semitic word signifying "reed" or "straight like reeds." A "canon," literally, was a straight rod or bar that kept something straight. It could refer to staves that preserved the shape of the shield, a weaver's rod to which alternate threads of the warp were attached, a line used by masons or carpenters, a ruler, beam of the balance, curtain rod, and bed posts. In art it was a standard or model; in grammar, a general rule; in history, a table of dates; in geography, a boundary. Before placing tiles on a floor, today, homeowners are asked to make a chalk line that then becomes the line at which the first line of tiles are placed. Consecutive tiles then are placed to the right or left of that first set of tiles. Thus, a chalk line would be a "canon." In the same way, the Bible is a canon or standard by which believers evaluate their own lives.

Even as one tile by itself cannot be a measure by which to determine another tile, Paul says that people cannot measure themselves by looking at one another. They must use "the standard (canon) measure with which the God of measure apportioned" (10:13). God's standard for measure is what matters. Therefore, to seek to be approved or included by those humans who commend themselves is of no usefulness at all. Paul, of course, alludes to this self-commendation in chapter 3. In chapter 10 he uses the extended metaphor of measuring space as a springboard to discuss some people who were apportioning "territory" that was not theirs. That "territory" is receiving credit for "work done by others" (10:15–16). If people seek to satisfy God's canon measure in their work among others, then indeed they can be sure they will be declared "approved" by the Lord.

Verse 18 is a very practical verse by which to guide daily actions and long-range plans. Does my action please God? When I bow before the Lord at judgment will God say: "I am well pleased with you. Stand up and be crowned!" Will the

Lord commend us? Humans, on the other hand, find themselves tending to submit to the pressures of humans who commend others, using these as a standard. Paul is certainly not against following the model of devout believers (e.g., Phil. 3:17; 1 Cor. 4:16–17), but the follower must always remember that other humans are models only insofar as they follow God's standards.

B. Paul Explains His Style of Work (11:12–12:18)

Although Paul has described something of the manner in which he and his coworkers work in chapter 10 (waging war for their Ruler-God and measuring by God's standard), his emphasis has been to explain how they do *not* work (waging war as the world does, inconsistency between the words in presence and in absence, and measuring oneself with oneself). The "foolishness" Paul introduces in chapter 11 is the need Paul has to defend his ministry more directly.

1. The Wise Fool and the Foolish Wise (11:1–6).

For a dearly beloved family member to defend his foundational principles is indeed foolishness. Nevertheless, the Corinthians have forced Paul to do so. So, Paul uses the analogy of a father and daughter. An ancient father would arrange the marriage and give away the daughter to the groom, similarly, Paul, as the person who introduced the Corinthians to Jesus the Messiah, is a spiritual parent. "I have a zeal for you with a zeal of God" (11:2) aptly describes not only Paul's earnest concern for the Corinthians but also Paul's zeal for everything he did in life. When he did not believe in the Messiah, he zealously persecuted Christians. When he did believe in the Messiah, he zealously served Christians. Paul, as any loving father, has concern for the well-being of his daughter. Paul "promised in marriage" the Corinthians (individuals who make up *one* entity) as a pure virgin to "one husband, to Christ" (11:2). Many ancient engagements required a year of preparation in which both the bride and the groom would save their funds for the forthcoming marriage (Mishnah Ket. 5:2). The book of Revelation uses similar imagery when teaching about a forthcoming marriage supper of the Lamb (Rev. 19:7–9).

Paul explicitly confronts the Corinthians at this time.

Consistent with his imagery, he compares the Corinthians with Eve who "was deceived by the serpent's cunning" (11:3). Paul is afraid that the Corinthians "*may* be led astray" from their "sincere and pure devotion to Christ." Paul uses the subjunctive mood to indicate that the Corinthians have not yet completely disobeyed God as Eve eventually did. They stand like Eve, admiring the tree of the knowledge of good and evil (Gen. 2:9; 3:6). Knowledge has always been such a temptation to the Corinthians. (Paul also was to use the analogy of Eve to the Ephesians who also desired to be great "teachers of the law" [1 Tim. 2:14; 1:7].)

The sexual purity that God requires of the bride and groom would be analogous to the spiritual purity of believers. Paul had used another pleonasm in 1:12 to describe the behavior of Paul and his coworkers toward the Corinthians—one of "holiness and sincerity." Paul and his coworkers had a purity of motive toward the Corinthians. The churches of Macedonia also were sincere and open-hearted ("generous" 8:2), even as a garment without folds is simple and self-evident. But were the Corinthians similarly "sincere" and "pure"? Was their repentance complete?

Would a sincere and pure fianceé become devoted to another man? Yet, Paul believes, the Corinthians (although they might not "put up with" Paul's defense) certainly seem to "put up with" people who "preach a Jesus other than the Jesus [Paul and his coworkers] preached," "receive a different spirit from the one [the Corinthians] received," or accept "a different gospel from the one [they] accepted" (11:1, 4). To whom does Paul refer? He refers to the "super-apostles," the "beyond measure-apostles." They masquerade as apostles of Christ, but, in reality, they are servants of Satan (11:13–15).

2. Salary as Ministry (11:7–15).

The reader now understands that the Corinthian charge that Paul is "lowly" ("timid" NIV, 10:1) means that Paul is too "lowly" to charge the Corinthians for his ministry (11:7). However, Paul used money as a means to advance people's spiritual growth. In a passionate defense in 1 Corinthians 9:1–18 Paul pointed out that he and Barnabas, like Peter, the Lord's brothers, and the other apostles had the right to be paid for their teaching. Paul saw nothing inherently wrong in being paid for preaching, as some commentators mistakenly suggest. He took up his trade of tentmaking whenever he wanted to impress a point on a congregation. For example, he did not accept any money from the Corinthians because the Corinthians appeared to be afraid that Paul and Barnabas were out to take advantage of them (1 Cor. 9:6; 2 Cor. 12:13–18). Furthermore, the false apostles had confused the Corinthians, convincing them that one of the criteria of true apostleship was receiving money. Ironically, then, when the false apostles were taking financial advantage of the Corinthians they were by their standards proving their apostleship (2 Cor. 2:17; 11:12).

The Corinthians both feared being taken advantage of financially and desired to pay in order to prove the recipient's worth. Since their view of money was so completely warped, Paul did not want to allow the Corinthians to support him financially. Such a move would have confirmed the false apostles and undermined what Paul was trying to teach the Corinthians. As Acts 18:5 testifies, Paul stopped working in Corinth only when Timothy and Silas arrived from Macedonia.

For another example, Paul did not allow the Thessalonians to support him financially, but for different reasons. For their edification, he, Timothy, and Silas worked among them in order to show that a person does well to work with his hands. So in 1 Thessalonians 5:14 he writes, "And we urge you, brothers, warn those who are idle," and in 4:11–12, "Make it your ambition to lead a quiet life, to mind your own business, and to work with your hands . . . so that you will not be dependent on anybody." Thus, in 2 Thessalonians he can command them to "keep away from every brother who is idle" because:

> We were not idle when we were with you, nor did we eat anyone's food without paying for it. On the contrary, we worked night and day, laboring and toiling so that we would not be a burden to any of you. We did this, not because we do not have the right to such help, but in order to make ourselves a model for you to follow. For even when we were with you, we gave you this rule: "If a man will not work, he shall not eat" (2 Thess. 3:6–10).

Therefore, to be allowed to contribute financially to Paul and his ministry was a privilege. As far as the Bible tells us, the Philippians were the only church that consistently was allowed by Paul to help him financially. What does that tell us about the Philippians? They had a healthy view of money. They did not hesitate to work. When they contributed to a person's ministry, they did not feel enslaved by that giving nor did they feel that paying a church worker a salary is being exploitative. And, conversely, they did not believe that financial remuneration proved a person's worth or authenticity, as happens sometimes in our cultures when people are valued by how much salary they get.

The Philippians had suffered as Paul had and they had grown to a position of equality with him, partnered with him in a way no other congregation was. As 2 Corinthians 8:1–2 indicates, the churches of Macedonia had suffered a severe affliction at least five years earlier and were now in extreme poverty. The Romans had been severe with them, taking possession of their gold and silver mines, felling their timber for the building of Roman ships, and reserving for themselves the import of salt. According to the Roman historian Livy who lived from 59 B.C. to A.D. 17:

> The unexpected grant of freedom cheered men, as well as the lightening of the annual taxation; but to those who were cut off from trading between regions, their country seemed as mangled as an animal disjointed into parts, each of which needed the other; so unaware were the Macedonians themselves of the size of Macedonia, of how it lent itself to divisions, and of how self-sufficient each part was (Livy 45:30).

Nevertheless, not only did the Philippians give, but they were very generous, while the Corinthians in contrast had financial abundance (2 Cor. 8:14) and were hesitant. Of course, not everyone at Philippi was necessarily poor. Lydia of Thyatira, who insisted on housing Paul and Silas when they were in Philippi (Acts 16:15, 40), was a dealer in purple cloth. Purple dye was expensive. As the most valued of ancient dyes, it was a sign of power, used to honor a king or designate a king's wealth. Extensive capital was needed to trade in such an expensive commodity and dealers in purple cloth were well-to-do. No doubt Lydia was a generous contributor toward Paul's support, but as a group, the Philippians were poor, even if individuals among them were wealthy. But whether poor or rich, the Philippians were generous. They had a proper attitude toward money, an attitude Paul longed for the Corinthians to emulate.

3. Paul's ironic boasting (11:16–28).

Paul does not want to be foolish, but if being "foolish" attracts the Corinthians, he is willing to be foolish. Many people "are boasting according to the flesh" ("boasting in the way the world does" 11:18). Paul too will "boast," but he never says that he will boast "according to the flesh." In fact, he does not really boast at all.

When Søren Kierkegaard writes to the religious but insincere church of Denmark of his time, he uses primarily indirect communication. Direct communication "presupposes that the receiver's ability to receive is undisturbed":

> For there is an immense difference, a dialectical difference between these two cases: the case of a man who is ignorant and is to have a piece of knowledge imparted to him, so that he is like an empty vessel which is to be filled or a blank sheet of paper upon which something is to be written; and the case of a man who is under an illusion and must first be delivered from that.[3]

Paul has been writing to people "under an illusion." In chapter 11 Paul intensifies the dramatic irony of his words to try to break through the Corinthian illusion—their admiration for false apostles. The meaning Paul intends to communicate purposely conflicts with the language and tone he uses. Paul wants to bring out the incongruities that occur between the reality and the appearances of the behavior of the Corinthians. He also uses verbal irony many times. When a speaker uses a word(s) to express a meaning directly opposite from the literal meaning, he or she is using verbal irony. "Irony" comes from the Greek *eirōneia*, ignorance purposely affected to provoke or

---

[3] Kierkegaard, Søren, *The Point of View for My Work as an Author*, trans. Walter Lowrie (New York: Harper, 1962), p. 40.

confound an antagonist. "*Super*-apostle" is irony. Paul intends to say the opposite—"*inferior*-apostle" (11:5).[4]

The Corinthians consider themselves wise (11:19; 1 Cor. 4:10); however, in Paul's estimation, they are misled. Paul asks the Corinthians to receive him as a "fool" so that (as a fool and before fools) he, too, may have an opportunity to boast. What Paul is really saying is that only fools boast and that the Corinthians only listen to fools who boast. The Corinthians are not wise at all to desire sadistic leaders and believe that the gentle, loving Paul is the unwise person.

Paul sets up a comparison between two types of boasting: boasting "the way the world does" and ironic boasting (boasting that shows that God must be at work in one's life). Paul allows the Corinthians to keep identifying themselves as "wise," but he attacks that self-perception indirectly as he describes exactly what is entailed in the wisdom of the Corinthians: wisdom to allow enslavement, exploitation, theft, rejection, and physical abuse. By repeating "if anyone" five times Paul, as it were, explosively, repeatedly lists these shocking signs of "wisdom." The Corinthians "are patient if anyone enslaves [them], if anyone exploits, if anyone takes advantage, if anyone puts on airs, if anyone slaps [them] in the face" (11:20). The Corinthian "wise" are patient even with their own enslavement!

Paul uses images of slavery, eating, hunting, and lifting to describe the type of leadership the Corinthians unwisely seek. When one eats, hunts, and enslaves, the object loses its life. Similarly, the super-apostles' impressive, arrogant, and sadistic leadership will result in the spiritual death of the Corinthians. Is "strength" the opposite of meekness and gentleness (11:21; 10:1)? Was Paul "too weak" to treat the Corinthians as a slave trader, exploiter, robber, and beater? Paul states his response in irony. He and his coworkers were not to Paul's shame "too weak," but rather, to his credit "too strong"!

Paul shifts the focus from "boasting" to "daring" in 11:21b:

---

[4]For a developed exposition of 2 Corinthians 11:16–12:10, see Aída Besançon Spencer, "The Wise Fool (and the Foolish Wise): A Study of Irony in Paul," *Novum Testamentum* XXIII, 4 (1981), 349–360, and *Paul's Literary Style: A Stylistic and Historical Comparison of 2 Corinthians 11:16–12:13, Romans 8:9–39, and Philippians 3:2–4:13*, Evangelical Theological Society Monograph (Winona Lake: Eisenbrauns, 1984), pp. 133–221.

"wherein anyone is being bold, in foolishness I say, I also am being bold." Paul now removes the weapons of attack and grabs the weapons of defense (6:7). Paul wants the Corinthians to see exactly how he and these "super-apostles" compare as genuine leaders. In four brief parallel questions, Paul easily matches the claims the super-apostles flaunt:

Hebrews are they? I also.

Israelites are they? I also.

Seed of Abraham are they? I also (11:22).

Paul emphasizes the claims by placing the direct objects first: Hebrews, Israelites, seed of Abraham. These three phrases are all synonyms with only possibly subtle differences in meaning: people who speak Hebrew, people with Hebrew religious training, people with a common race.[5] A quick "I also" answers the challenge, thereby placing little significance on these claims. The questions take on an increasing cadence that moves the reader quickly to verse 23: "Servants of Christ are they?" Finally, Paul breaks the parallelism because as "servants of Christ" Paul and the super-apostles are not parallel: "Being out of my mind I am speaking, I even more." Again Paul uses "out of my mind" ironically. He does not think he is mentally immature or unbalanced, but he writes in this defensive way that he would prefer to avoid in order to help a "mentally immature" Corinthian church to comprehend the truth.

"I even more," Paul writes, omitting the verb "am" and the second half of the sentence, "a servant of Christ than they are." By omitting the end of his sentence, Paul forces the reader to be caught up in a description of Paul's life before knowing exactly what Paul intends to communicate by this list of trials. Paul requires his readers to pause and reflect on the missing words: "I [am] even more [a servant of Christ than they are]." Paul will extensively illustrate what it means to be a "servant of Christ." How is Paul a greater "servant of Christ"? He is: "in troubles to a greater degree, in prisons to a greater degree, in misfortunes to a much greater degree, in death many times" (11:23). The irony rests in these happenings being cause for "boasting." Certainly these difficulties would not impress the "superlative" apostles.

[5] Héring, Jean. *The Second Epistle of Saint Paul to the Corinthians*, trans. A. W. Heathcote and P. J. Allcock (London: Epworth, 1967), p. 83 n. 24.

Yet Paul's goal is not to impress them; rather, it is to *teach* them what authentic leadership is all about. No one can boast about difficulties if God is the one who sustains a human in those difficulties.

Paul uses a marked and hurried rhythm as he describes his many troubles. Images of prisons and death create a bleak picture indeed. Paul uses several adverbs to accentuate the picture: "greater degree, much greater degree, many times, five times, forty less one, three times, once, a day and a night." The verbs are vivid: "beaten, stoned, suffered shipwreck." "Dangers" occurs eight times in chapter 11. That one word aptly describes much of Paul's life. Paul has had to experience every kind of danger from nature, from people, from nonbelievers, and from so-called believers. Paul pairs off rivers and robbers, kin and Gentiles, city, wilderness, sea and false brothers. The pleonasm "trouble and hardship" also summarizes and emphasizes what Paul has had to endure for the Lord's sake (11:27).

Finally, Paul's list that began in 11:23 ends abruptly in 11:28 with the clause: "Apart from what I leave unmentioned [there is] the daily pressure on me, the concern for all the churches." Can it be possible after all these experiences that Paul has left something "unmentioned"? Paul's illustrations are indeed endless. Previously he has described physical discomfort from persecution and from traveling about in order to proclaim Christ. Now he adds mental anguish as well because of his responsibility and passionate concern for the spiritual well-being of believers. The image of "pressure" well describes this new hardship. Even as a physical pressure can cause long-term discomfort, similarly concern for the well-being of others has caused Paul long-term mental discomfort.

Paul's "boasting" is no boasting at all. Paul has listed the difficulties he has been enduring to show the kind of life that proves the genuineness of a servant of Christ. Only for the sake of Christ would anyone endure such difficulties.

4. Weakness (11:29–12:10).

In 11:29 Paul first uses "weak" in a positive way to describe himself. A "weak" person might be someone tempted to sin. Such people would cause Paul to be anxious (11:28). Paul would identify with the tempted person and be indignantly angry against those who caused this fall.

Paul uses "weakness" in 11:30 as an internal summary word to describe a servant of Christ: "If I must boast, I will boast of the things that show my weakness." This verse and 12:9 ("my power is made perfect in weakness") are often used to show that God works in a person with "weaknesses" or moral defects. In other words, Paul would be speaking in 2 Corinthians of his personal deficiencies or sins. For example, John Calvin, one of the founders of the Protestant Reformation, says that "weakness" in 12:10 includes personal deficiencies.[6] Philip Edgcumbe Hughes says that weakness refers to a human's decaying physical frame.[7] Others have suggested that "weakness" refers to physical illness. "Weakness" (*astheneō*) literally refers to lack of physical strength. In the Gospels it often refers to sickness (e.g., Matt. 8:17; Luke 5:15), but Paul uses *astheneō* metaphorically. The verb, noun, and adjective (*astheneō, astheneia, asthenēs*) are used metaphorically to refer to "weakness" forty-five times in the New Testament, thirty-nine times by Paul, thirty times in 1 and 2 Corinthians. It occurs fifteen times in 2 Corinthians 10–13.

Although people need to repent of their wrongdoings (e.g., Luke 18:9–14) and acknowledge their limitations so that God can empower them (Exod. 4:10–12), Paul does not use "weakness" to refer to sins or psychological limitations in this passage. Rather, Paul employs "weakness" in 2 Corinthians 11–12 to refer to the physical and mental discomfort he has had to endure as part of his desire to preach the good news of Christ. Weakness is physical discomfort due to persecution, physical discomfort due to traveling about and encountering natural disasters and robbery, physical discomfort from hard work and living without all physical necessities, and mental anguish from responsibility for the churches (11:23–29). Paul's escape from Damascus is another example of danger he had to incur because

[6]Calvin, John. *Calvin's Commentaries: Romans—Galatians* (Wilmington: Associated Publishers and Authors, [n.d.]), p. 1846.

[7]Hughes, Philip Edgcumbe, *Paul's Second Epistle to the Corinthians, New International Commentary on the New Testament* (Grand Rapids: Eerdmans, 1962), p. 418.

he preached Christ (11:32–33). People who live the way "the world does" (10:3) might see such discomfort as "sickness." Unlike the arrogance and desire for comfort of the "super-apostles," Paul lived this difficult but unflamboyant life of self-sacrifice. To interpret "weakness" as individual personality traits dilutes the power of what Paul claims. To reinterpret "weakness" as individual traits might allow an interpreter to live more comfortably, whereas Paul's use of "weakness" requires the willingness to take risks and the possibility of a change of lifestyle. Verse 30 can be rephrased: "If I must boast [i.e., find something that is a sign of a true servant of Christ], I will boast of a life of affliction for the sake of Christ which is looked down upon by others."

Paul then speaks of himself in the third person ("I know a man in Christ") because although the Corinthians might very well be impressed by his visions and revelations, such flashy events are not what they should look for when trying to find the genuine servant of Christ: "I will boast" only "about my weaknesses" (12:5).

Paul's passionate discussion of "weakness" reaches a climax in 12:9 when God says to Paul: "'My grace is sufficient for you, for my power is made perfect in weakness,'" and Paul says, "Therefore, I will boast all the more gladly about my weaknesses, so that Christ's power may rest on me." Paul has taken a negative word used to criticize him and reinterpreted it in a positive way so that he can even say he "gladly" boasts in weaknesses.

The "weaknesses" include the "thorn in the flesh" (12:7). Since Paul writes here metaphorically, commentators have disagreed as to its referent. Paul draws a picture of a thorn or splinter that hits or pierces the flesh. He also pictures a messenger of Satan who strikes him with a fist, as a boxer would knock someone about. In other words, the "thorn to or in the flesh" seems to be an external, localized problem rather than an internal one. Some commentators have suggested that the "thorn" could be an individual or a specific persecution, but probably most commentators are correct in seeing the "thorn" as some kind of physical suffering. Elsewhere in the New Testament Paul speaks of some intermittent eye problem such as ophthalmia, which evoked scorn from some people (Gal. 4:13–15; 6:11).[8] Paul correctly saw such physical suffering as part of the Satanic dominion. God does not remove permanently this physical suffering from Paul because God wants Paul to learn that he can still function perfectly in ministry and in life.

God's grace is sufficient for Paul because God imparts strength and power to the person who looks weak or powerless. Paul's "weaknesses" are the "insults," "hardships," "persecutions," and "difficulties" he undergoes as a part of his ministry. And when Paul willingly lives this life of difficulties for the greater cause to advance God's reign, Christ's power comes down to Paul as the shekinah glory descended upon the mercy-seat in the Tabernacle, and "takes up its abode" (12:9).[9] Paul ends his discussion with the paradox: "At the time that I am not strong, then I am strong" (12:10). Power cannot come unless preceded by weakness (humility of life?). Power is what the Corinthians want. They want a burdensome and powerful presence to match a powerful writer (10:10). However, Paul wants them to know that the power the Corinthians desire will never be reached by the means they use—obedience toward those who flaunt their authority and who live for comfort.

How then can we discern the false from the genuine Christian leader? The false Christian despises a life of danger, physical discomfort from persecutions, insults, calamities, frequent nearness to death, infirmities, and mental anguish for the sake of Christ. When Paul was chosen along the road to Damascus, Jesus told Ananias that Paul was chosen "to carry my name before the Gentiles and their kings and before the people of Israel. I will show him how much he must suffer for my name" (Acts 9:15–16). Paul discovered that some people thought his difficulties were a sign of his lack of power. Paul learned that his difficulties were an opportunity for God to work through him. Paul could "boast" in difficulties not because he

---

[8] Plummer, Alfred, *A Critical and Exegetical Commentary on the Second Epistle to the Corinthians*, International Critical Commentary (Edinburgh: T. & T. Clark, 1915), pp. 350–51. Dr. Stephen Price, a general practitioner in Hamilton, Massachusetts, has suggested that Paul's eye symptoms could more specifically have been the inflammatory Reiter's condition (which also affects the joints) or intermittent glaucoma that causes the eye pressure to rise at times.

[9] Hughes, p. 452.

liked difficulties or because he thought he had more stamina than anyone else, but because his difficulties proved that God was at work in his life and that Paul's intentions were sincere.

5. The problems (12:11–18).

After a letter that has moved concentrically from less to more direct communication, Paul concludes this section with a direct elaboration of the problems he and the Corinthians have with each other. The Corinthians compelled Paul to be "foolish"—in other words, to defend himself, although they should have been defending Paul themselves. Paul is "not in the least inferior to the 'super-apostles'" (12:11). Paul has exhibited all the "supernatural" types of miracles such as healing and exorcism that cause people to repent (12:12; e.g., Acts 19:11–12; Matt. 11:20). Paul and his associates refused to accept money from the Corinthians although the Corinthians might see this salary as confirmation of Paul's apostleship (12:13–16). They wanted no opportunity for the Corinthians to confuse their work with the work of false, self-seeking persons.

C. Paul Summarizes His Defense (12:19–13:11)

Now Paul brings his concerns specifically to the case in point. What has preceded has been a preparation of the Corinthians to receive Paul. "Have you been thinking," he asks in 12:19, "that we have been defending ourselves to you?" Have the Corinthians been lulled by his apology into supposing that Paul has entered into some kind of public political debate with the pseudo-apostles, vying for the loyalty of the Corinthians? Paul denies fervently that this has been his aim. Illuminating his intention in chapters 1–5, he explains that what he has been doing in the sight of God through his defense is ministering to the Corinthians, preparing them for his visit so that they will eliminate the division, slander, arrogance, and sexual impurity that has been rampant among them—the sinful climate that has allowed the false apostles like noxious weeds to flourish in their midst. The false apostles are now revealed not to be a cause of Paul's problems with the Corinthians. They are but a symptom of the continual problem of the Corinthians' spiritual health. Paul has only addressed the false apostles' accusations as a means to minister to the deeper seated spiritual problems of the troubled Corinthians, problems that allowed the slander of the pseudo-apostles to fester among them. Like a good gardener, Paul will come and root these noxious growths out of his field; but, of more concern to him, he will till that field, filling it full of good nourishment that will allow healthy spiritual fruit to flourish. Twice he has been among the Corinthians. Now for a third time, he will return (13:1), this time with a "strong" personal agenda, for "he will not spare those who sinned earlier" (13:2).

Have there been complaints about Paul's presence with the inference that Christ is not present in his ministry? "On my return I will not spare those who sinned earlier or any of the others," Paul writes in 13:2–3, "since you are demanding proof that Christ is speaking through me." Again, picking up the word "weakness" that has been hurled in accusation against him he writes literally: "But [Christ] is not weak among you but strong in you. For even he was crucified out of weakness, but he lives out of strength of God. For we also are weak in him, but we will live with him in [the] strength of God among you" (13:3–4). Paralleling his style with Christ's, Paul warns that he will manifest the power that the sinful seek by punishing them powerfully. How does what Paul declared in verses 3–4 relate to his previous definitions of weakness? In relation to sin, in dealing with the Corinthians, Paul and Timothy are "strong." In their lifestyle they are "weak." Like Christ who was crucified in weakness, they live out of the strength of God. Thus, alert Corinthians would infer that to be a servant of Christ, one must live in weakness (risking suffering for Christ's sake) so that God's strength may indwell. Unalert Corinthians will be startled to find Paul not "as you want me to be" (12:20) and capable, though he wishes not to be, of being harsh in wielding his authority (13:10). The warning is clear. Christ lived a life of difficulties, dangers, persecutions, insults, calamities. He was frequently near death. Yet God empowered him continually, even to a glorious resurrection (e.g., 4:14).

Test yourselves against Christ's example, Paul counsels in 13:5–6. The Corinthians may fail, but Paul hopes that they will recognize that he and his coworkers have not failed to imitate

Christ. That proof of the presence of Christ that was challenged by Paul's accusers is displayed in a life withstanding the sufferings Christ endured, and through them experiencing the power of God that Christ manifested. Why does Paul undergo such suffering? Has not Jesus' death been sufficient so that Christians do not have to suffer? Paul's purpose is didactic. Someone once said that we are the only Jesus that many people will ever see. Christ-in-us is the ministry that models Jesus' example for the world. Model on me, Paul once counseled the Corinthians, as I model on Christ (1 Cor. 4:16; 11:1).

At first glance, verse 13:9 might be mistaken as a final ironic shot by Paul: "We are glad whenever we are weak but you are strong; and our prayer is for your perfection" (literally, completion, improvement). Perhaps Paul is being satirical. But nothing surrounding this verse is ironic. Paul instead is revealing his didactic intention. Paul's entreaty to change, culminating in 13:11, summarizes his charges in chapters 6–12 to "mend your ways," through plea and through example. All of his effort is for the Corinthians' edification and upbuilding. He has modeled Christ for them so that they might enjoy the power of God. Even if Paul is judged by the Corinthians to have failed, and they seek to better his modeling on Christ, he is pleased (13:7). All of his actions, even his receipt of authority, have been for the purpose of building up the saints (13:10). How truly he has emulated the Suffering Servant, displaying the greatest love that is possible to give in his willingness to suffer and eventually lay down his life for the churches.

For Further Study

1. Take *Young's* or *Strong's Concordance* and trace words such as "foolish" and "foolishness," "wise" and "wisdom," "weak," "out of one's mind," and "humble" or "lowly" in 1 and 2 Corinthians. In what different ways does Paul use these words?

2. Paul willingly underwent a life of suffering on behalf of the Corinthians. Must all Christians do that?

3. Paul points out the difference between those peddling the gospel for gain and his own self-sacrificing style of service.

What self-sacrificing servants of Christ do you know? What makes their ministries like Paul's? How can you emulate them?

4. Paul fought pagans and Judaizing believers to protect the Corinthians. Do any threaten us today?

5. What do you think of when you hear the word "strong"? Compare your gut-level thoughts with Paul's definition of strength. Name one action you can do to become "stronger" in a biblical sense.

Chapter 6

Final Greetings
(2 Corinthians 13:12–14)

As he closes, what does Paul want the Corinthians to take with them out of this searing epistle? When we began our analysis, we noted that the themes Paul develops were introduced in his opening greetings. In a similar way, the final thoughts he wishes his recipients to remember are often enclosed in his epistles' final moments. Whenever these letters were read aloud, the hearers were left with the point Paul wanted to make ringing in their ears. In this letter we have seen that the final paragraph begins with an injunction to "mend your ways" (RSV), to pay attention to Paul's appeal, to stop fighting with one another, and to live in peace with one another so that the God of love and peace can dwell among you. Now, as he enters his farewell, Paul expands the tones of the last phrase into greater and greater concentric circles.

A. Closing Benediction (13:12–14)

The first circle begins in the immediate; that is, from one Christian to a neighboring Christian. He urges: greet one another with an act of peace, the holy kiss. In ancient times the kiss of fellowship was a common sign of good will. Justin Martyr, the great Christian philosopher-teacher who lived from A.D. 100–165, just one hundred years after Paul, defended Christianity to the Emperor Hadrian against charges of cannibalism and immorality. In his *First Apology* he describes the earliest church service we have on record. After discussing the readings, the hymns, the sermon, the prayers, and the Amen, he notes, "On finishing the prayers we greet each other with a kiss" (65).

Today we could compare the kiss with shaking hands, although the former was more affectionate. It was given to persons of the same sex. Jews would kiss as a courteous preliminary to any ceremonious meal (e.g., Luke 7:45). For Christians it expressed the unity or fellowship of the Holy Spirit in the bond of peace (Rom. 16:16; 1 Cor. 16:20; 1 Peter 5:14). At the beginning of the Eucharist (from *eucharistia*, thanksgiving) or Lord's Supper, the kiss indicated peace or reconciliation between members of the congregation. Thus when Paul urged, "Greet one another with a holy kiss," he was entreating that they be reconciled to one another so that they might indicate it by the sign of reconciliation. By the 200s in the East the deacon would ask at the time of the kiss, "Is there any one who has anything against his fellow?" as a final precaution by the overseer before communion to make peace between them (Apostolic Tradition 2.18). This, then, is the first circle: that the Corinthians be reconciled one with another.

The next circle expands out with the next phrase, "All the saints send their greetings." Paul has sounded again and again his theme of economic familial interdependence among the churches. Now he reminds the churches one last time that there are other Christians around them who take an interest in them. What saints specifically does he have in mind? No doubt Paul means the Macedonians with whom he has just been ministering and whose example he has held continually up before the Corinthians, some of whom he may even bring with him to receive the Corinthian collection. "All the saints send their greetings" is to make the Corinthians aware again of the Christian church surrounding them. They are to remember they are but one part of a unifying whole, and they ought to contribute to the good of that whole.

Finally, Paul ends with the greatest circle of all, the one in which we live and move and have our being, as he reminded the Athenians (Acts 17:28): "May the grace of the Lord Jesus Christ, and the love of God, and the fellowship of the Holy Spirit be with you all." The great divine family, the unified Trinity, the God who is three-in-one is in relationship with all of the

Corinthians. From single believers, to the church of all believers, to the great engulfing, surrounding love of the triune God-head, Paul draws a powerful picture of the connecting bonds of love that embrace the Corinthians. How could they not respond to such a portrait of their true status?

B. Effect of 2 Corinthians (13:14ff.)

Poignant, passionate, compelling—2 Corinthians is a masterpiece of persuasive literature. It avoids being manipulative in that it is others-oriented, not motivated by personal gain as so many appeals made to us in the name of religion turn out to be, and not demanding a specific donation from each recipient. But—did the letter work? In the preface at the very outset of our study we noted that 2 Corinthians was the proof that the advice in 1 Corinthians was not heeded by all. In 2 Corinthians was it heeded? Did the Corinthians mend their ways and reconcile with one another, with Paul, and with the gospel of Jesus Christ? Have you ever wondered? We know the answer.

In Romans 15:26 Paul writes to tell the Romans that "Macedonia and Achaia were pleased to make a contribution for the poor among the saints in Jerusalem." He had in his hand their donation, positive proof of their willingness to be partners with him and to be true servants of Christ.

Another fascinating piece of evidence corroborates the notion that this attitude shift in the Corinthians was permanent and not simply one more of their infamous flights of fancy. In his letter to the Philippians (4:3) Paul writes, I ask you to "help these women (Euodia and Syntyche) who have contended at my side in the cause of the gospel, along with Clement and the rest of my fellow workers, whose names are in the book of life." Origen tells us that Clement became the third bishop of Rome. Eusebius also tells us that Linus was the first bishop appointed by Peter, then Anencletus for twelve years. Then Clement, who had become a leader in the Roman community, was appointed and served for nine years before he died, in the third year of Trajan's reign (Eusebius, *History of the Church* 3:4, 15, 34). If Clement died in A.D. 101, that would only have been four years after John returned to Ephesus from exile on Patmos when he received the vision he wrote down in Revelation (A.D. 96). In

Clement, if he is indeed the Clement of Philippians 4:3, we have someone who knew Paul and would no doubt have known the very Corinthians with whom Paul contended.

Clement, overseer at Rome, wrote a letter from the Church at Rome to the Church at Corinth in approximately A.D. 96. From this we speculate that if Origen and Eusebius are correct, we have a letter from a New Testament coworker of Paul who had gone on to shepherd the church at Rome and who would have known the very Corinthians with whom Paul worked. These Corinthians were spiritual (and no doubt, in many cases, physical) descendants at Corinth. Hence, A.D. 96 would be forty years after the events in Corinth sparked the writing of 2 Corinthians in A.D. 56.

What was happening about A.D. 96? Nineteen years had passed since the earthquake of 77, and the city had climbed out of the rubble to reopen commerce. Yet another sort of quake had shaken the Christian community. For fifteen years the cruel tyrant, Emperor Domitian, had persecuted the church. He had banished John to Patmos. The church was suffering sporadic persecution. Clement's letter exudes an apocalyptic sense of exile, fitting for an epistle circulating in the time when a monster ravished the church and John received his vision of Revelation. As Clement opens his letter "to the church of God, exiled in Corinth," we are struck by his description of the Corinthians. Clement compliments the Corinthian church on its reputation for excellence and firmness of faith. Apparently, Corinth had firmly made its decision to stand steadfastly with Paul and the other churches. Clement compliments the Corinthians on their sensible and considerate Christian piety, a compliment that would please Paul vastly. He honors them for their hospitality! Can these be the descendants of those same Corinthians who met Paul with cold disdain? He compliments their perfect and trustworthy knowledge. As we saw, knowledge was always and now still remained important to the Corinthians (1 Cor. 1:5). Clement praises the Corinthians' impartiality. (How Paul and his team members would have cheered!) Finally, and perhaps along with their generous hospitality the most delightful of all, he praises the Corinthians for their disciplined young people and blameless women with pure conscience—

women who treat their husbands with affection and are known for homes run with dignity and discretion (1 Clement 1:2–3).

What an improvement over the Corinth of "Corinthianize" whose morally flabby ancestors Paul exhorted in 2 Corinthians. Could Paul have recognized any aspect of the church that he knew? No doubt he could have when he saw the occasion for the letter. The Church at Corinth was in a state of revolt. A group of the young in the faith had taken over the church and deposed the elders. These were indeed the heirs of the same contentious Corinthians that Paul knew. They may have cleaned up their actions in regard to morality, generosity, impartiality, and the deportment of their children and women, but they were still the same contentious, factionalizing lot. (Some things remain constant.) Yet, Paul's good work had made great shifts in the church's attitudes. Did Clement's letter work? When this final lapse was brought to the church's attention by Clement, apparently Paul's prayer for obedience was answered in the spirit of the church.

Hegesippus, who lived immediately after Clement from A.D. 100–180, writing about a journey around A.D. 155–156, recounts: "The Corinthian church continued in the true doctrine until Primus became bishop. I mixed with them on my voyage to Rome and spent several days with the Corinthians, during which we were refreshed with the true doctrine" (Eusebius, *History of the Church* 4:22). Some seventy years after Clement's death, Dionysius of Corinth, about A.D. 170, speaks of the honor in which the letter previously written by Clement was held in the church. He writes that it was read publicly along with a more recent letter of exhortation from Soter, bishop of Rome (Eusebius, *History of the Church,* 4:23). Together with Paul's letters and other exhortations by the churches, these epistles had become a constant reminder to the Corinthians and to us, their heirs, of the ways of an obedient life that serves our sisters and brothers, and honors our Lord Jesus Christ.

For Further Study

1. Find an edition of the apostolic or early Christian Fathers and read the *First Letter of Clement to the Corinthians*.

Compare the church's strengths and problems about forty–fifty years later with its situation during Paul's life.

2. Review the three circles of relationships Paul draws for the Corinthians in his closing benedictions. How do you and your church relate to the three dimensions of Christian interpersonal relations?

Resources for Further Study

References Cited

Bauer, Walter. *A Greek-English Lexicon of the New Testament*, trans., eds. William F. Arndt and F. Wilbur Gingrich. Chicago: University, 1957.

Betz, Hans Dieter. "Paul's Apology: II Corinthians 10–13 and the Socratic Tradition." *The Center for Hermeneutical Studies in Hellenistic and Modern Culture*. Colloquy 2, 1970. Berkeley: Center for Hermeneutical Studies, 1975.

Calvin, John. *Calvin's Commentaries: Romans—Galatians*. Wilmington: Associated Publishers and Authors, [n.d.].

Cullmann, Oscar. *Peter: Disciple—Apostle—Martyr: A Historical and Theological Study*, trans. Floyd V. Filson. Philadelphia: Westminster, 1953.

Danby, Herbert, trans. *The Mishnah*. Oxford: University, 1933.

Eusebius. *The History of the Church from Christ to Constantine*, trans. G. A. Williamson. Minneapolis: Augsburg, 1965.

Geography of Strabo IV, trans. H. L. Jones. Loeb Classical Library. New York: G. P. Putnam's, 1947.

Héring, Jean. *The Second Epistle of Saint Paul to the Corinthians*, trans. A. W. Heathcote and P. J. Allcock. London: Epworth, 1967.

Hughes, Philip E. *Paul's Second Epistle to the Corinthians*. The New International Commentary on the New Testament. Grand Rapids: Eerdmans, 1962.

James, Montague Rhodes. *The Apocryphal New Testament*. Oxford: Clarendon, 1924.

Jeremias, Joachim. *Jerusalem in the Time of Jesus: An Investigation into Economic and Social Conditions during the New Testament*

Period, trans. F. H. and C. H. Cave. 3rd ed. Philadelphia: Fortress, 1969.

Kepler, Thomas S., ed. *Contemporary Thinking About Paul: An Anthology.* New York: Abingdon-Cokesbury, 1950.

Keyes, Clinton W. "The Greek Letter of Introduction." *American Journal of Philology,* LVI (1935), 28–44.

Kierkegaard, Søren. *The Point of View for My Work as an Author,* trans. Walter Lowrie. New York: Harper, 1962.

Liddell, Henry George and Robert Scott. *A Greek-English Lexicon,* ed. Henry Stuart Jones. 9th ed. Oxford: Clarendon, 1940.

Livy XIII, trans. Alfred C. Schlesinger. Loeb Classical Library. Cambridge: Harvard University, 1968.

MacDonald, Greville. *George MacDonald and His Wife.* London: George Allen & Unwin, 1924.

Martin, Ralph P. *2 Corinthians.* Word Biblical Commentary, Vol. 40. Waco: Word, 1986.

Murphy-O'Connor, Jerome. *St. Paul's Corinth: Texts and Archaeology.* Good News Studies 6. Wilmington: Michael Glazier, 1983.

Philo, trans. F. H. Colson. 10 vols. Cambridge: Harvard University, 1941, 1949.

Plummer, Alfred. *Second Epistle of St. Paul to the Corinthians.* The International Critical Commentary. Edinburgh: T. & T. Clark, 1915.

Ramsay, W. M. *St. Paul the Traveller and the Roman Citizen.* New York: G. P. Putnam's Sons, 1896.

———. *The Cities of St. Paul: Their Influence on His Life and Thought.* New York: Armstrong, 1980.

Richardson, Cyril C., ed., trans. *Early Christian Fathers.* Library of Christian Classics, I. New York: Macmillan, 1970.

Robertson, A. T. *A Grammar of the Greek New Testament in the Light of Historical Research.* 4th ed. Nashville: Broadman, 1934.

Sherwin-White, Adrian Nicholas. *The Roman Citizenship.* 2nd ed. Oxford: Clarendon, 1973.

———. *Roman Society and Roman Law in the New Testament.* Oxford: Clarendon, 1963.

Spencer, Aída Besançon. *Paul's Literary Style: A Stylistic and Historical Comparison of II Corinthians 11:16–12:13, Romans 8:9–39, and Philippians 3:2–4:13.* Evangelical Theological Society Monograph. Winona Lake: Eisenbrauns, 1984.

———. "The Wise Fool (and the Foolish Wise): A Study of Irony in Paul." *Novum Testamentum,* 23 (October, 1981), 349–60.

Thayer, Joseph Henry. *Thayer's Greek-English Lexicon of the New Testament*. Marshallton: National Foundation for Christian Education, 1885.

Unnik, W. C. van. *Tarsus or Jerusalem: The City of Paul's Youth*, trans. George Ogg. London: Epworth, 1962.

Usher, Stephen, trans. *Dionysius of Halicarnassus: The Critical Essays I*. Loeb Classical Library. Cambridge: Harvard University, 1974.

Other Helpful References

Aune, David E. *The New Testament in its Literary Environment*. Philadelphia: Westminster, 1987.

Georgi, Dieter. *The Opponents of Paul in Second Corinthians*. Philadelphia: Fortress, 1986.

Hafemann, Scott J. *Suffering and the Spirit: An Exegetical Study of II Cor. 2:14–3:3 within the Context of the Corinthian Correspondence*. Wissenschaftliche Untersuchungen zum Neuen Testament 2. Reiche 19. Tuebingen: J. C. B. Mohr, 1986.

Meyer, Heinrich A W. *Critical and Exegetical Hand-Book to the Epistles of the Corinthians*. New York: Funk & Wagnalls, 1884.

Paphahatzis, Nicos. *Ancient Corinth: The Museums of Corinth, Isthmia and Sicyon*, trans. Kay Cicellis. Athens: Ekdotike Athenon, 1978.

Spencer, Aída Besançon and William David Spencer. "The Truly Spiritual in Paul: Biblical Paper on 1 Corinthians 2:6–16." *Conflict and Context: Hermaneutics in the Americas*, eds. Mark Lau Branson and C. René Padilla. Grand Rapids: Eerdmans, 1986.

Yaumauchi, Edwin M. *Pre-Christian Gnosticism: A Survey of the Proposed Evidence*. Grand Rapids: Eerdmans, 1973.

Young, Frances and David F. Ford. *Meaning and Truth in 2 Corinthians*. Grand Rapids: Eerdmans, 1987.